AI FIRST

The Playbook for a Future-Proof
Business and Brand

AI FIRST

Adam Brotman
Andy Sack

HARVARD BUSINESS REVIEW PRESS
BOSTON, MASSACHUSETTS

Copyright 2025 Harvard Business School Publishing Corporation

Printed in India by Replika Press Pvt. Ltd.

10 9 8 7 6 5

The web addresses referenced in this book were live and correct at the time of the book's publication but may be subject to change.

Library of Congress Cataloging-in-Publication Data

Names: Brotman, Adam, author. | Sack, Andy, author.
Title: AI first : the playbook for a future-proof business and brand /
    Adam Brotman and Andy Sack.
Description: Boston, Massachusetts : Harvard Business Review Press, [2025] |
    Includes bibliographical references and index.
Identifiers: LCCN 2024047958 (print) | LCCN 2024047959 (ebook) |
    ISBN 9781647829650 (hardcover) | ISBN 9781647829667 (epub)
Subjects: LCSH: Technological innovations—Management. |
    Artificial intelligence. | Organizational change.
Classification: LCC HD45 .B734 2025 (print) | LCC HD45 (ebook) |
    DDC 658.5/14—dc23/eng/20250206
LC record available at https://lccn.loc.gov/2024047958
LC ebook record available at https://lccn.loc.gov/2024047959

ISBN: 978-1-64782-965-0
eISBN: 978-1-64782-966-7

MIX
Paper | Supporting
responsible forestry
FSC
www.fsc.org   FSC™ C016779

We dedicate this book to our families—Alexa, Coco, and Jude (Andy), and Carrie and Addison (Adam)—because we love them and also because we choose to be optimistic about the net positives of AI and our collective future.

Contents

THE HOLY-SHIT MOMENT

I n October 2023, on a perfect, sunny Bay Area day, we found ourselves standing in the Franklin Square playground at the corner of Bryant and 17th in the heart of San Francisco, and about three blocks from the 101, the main artery to the heart of Silicon Valley. We were silent. For minutes we just looked at each other and tried to make sense of what we had just heard.

We were fresh out of a meeting with Sam Altman, the cofounder and CEO of OpenAI, at his company's offices. It started with Sam coming to greet us himself in the company's lobby, dressed in a bright-yellow hoodie, with bright yellow running shoes and a friendly, welcoming personality. We were there to explain how our company, Forum3, was building a platform for brands to help them implement AI-based solutions, particularly in the marketing and digital-engagement realm, and to get Sam's feedback on our direction.

Sam said he was a fan of what we had accomplished for Starbucks, referring to both Adam's tenure as Starbucks's chief digital officer, but also Forum3's work with Starbucks to envision and implement its latest Web3 loyalty offering, Starbucks Odyssey. And he indicated that he liked our company's new direction. But he admitted that he wasn't very familiar with consumer brand marketing and said that he was focused really on only one thing these days: achieving AGI.

It wasn't what we expected to hear. "AGI?" we asked. We knew that it stood for artificial general intelligence, and thought we understood it as a term referring generally to when the AI models could think for themselves, be super intelligent, and develop enough agency and smarts so that they could turn on humans, like in the movie *The Terminator*. He used the term AGI so smoothly and nonchalantly, as if we knew what he meant. But we hadn't studied AGI itself much yet, so we felt compelled to ask Sam, "When you say AGI, what do you mean?" We winced even as we asked it, given that it might seem like a dumb question to ask one of the most important AI leaders on the planet. But after pausing and thinking, Sam said, "That's a fair question, and I would say it's when AI will be able to achieve novel scientific breakthroughs on its own."

We replied, "OK, wow. That's sort of . . . wild. Not sure exactly what that means, but what do you think AGI will mean for us, and for consumer brand marketers trying to create ad campaigns and the like to build their companies?" It may have seemed like a sudden, lowbrow thing to ask after learning that AGI might cure cancer, but given how little time we had with Sam we felt like we had to bridge the conversation back to our specific realm of business.

"Oh, for that? It will mean that ninety-five percent of what marketers use agencies, strategists, and creative professionals for today will easily, nearly instantly, and at almost no cost be handled by the AI— and the AI will likely be able to test the creative against real or synthetic customer focus groups for predicting results and optimizing. Again, all free, instant, and nearly perfect. Images, videos, campaign ideas? No problem."

No words. We were nodding, processing.

"One last question," we asked finally. "About when do you think AGI will be a reality?"

"Five years," he replied, "give or take, maybe slightly longer—but no one knows exactly when or what it will mean for society."

. . .

After that meeting with Sam, it was clear that the book we were writing on digital transformation in the latest technology age needed to take a different path than we originally thought. Sort of like our company, Forum3.

We founded our company around the shared vision and conviction that we're entering a new convergent era of technology, with an already radically digitized landscape. We wanted to build a company and platform that would help consumer brands embrace and navigate these transformational changes to build their brands in this new era.

We started with Web3—which may already feel like it's past its freshness date. After envisioning, advising, and running a handful of Web3 projects during 2021, we were hired by Starbucks to help create Starbucks Odyssey, the loyalty and community project. The invite-only launch, in December 2022, went better than expected, with nearly a million people signing up for the waiting list. Odyssey is part collectible community, part game, part rewards program—a novel way to combine some of the best customer-engagement techniques under one roof. To play Odyssey, Starbucks Rewards members engage in a series of "brand journeys and activities" that allow members to learn more about the brand, earn digital collectibles, and level up in a new type of game that rewards them with coffee for a month, or custom tumblers with Starbucks heritage artwork, or something else.

So, Forum3 seemed to be doing what it set out to do. And yet months later, in the office of Sam Altman, talking about the future of AI and what it would mean for Forum3, we realized that we needed more than anything else to become an AI first company. How would that happen? Where was the pivot?

Well, right when Starbucks Odyssey launched, in December 2022, ChatGPT also launched to the public. It took about ten minutes of playing with ChatGPT-3.5 for us to realize that everything had changed. We were two supposed "digital thought leaders"—lifers in this world—and we were dumbfounded.

We met twenty years ago, in a peer-to-peer group for "young entrepreneurs." The Seattle chapter of this group placed each of us in a group they labeled as "Forum3." We have been close friends ever since. Andy went on to found multiple successful tech companies and seed venture funds, and ultimately to advise Microsoft CEO Satya Nadella and his team on digital innovation. Adam went on to be the chief digital officer of Starbucks and the president and co-CEO of J.Crew.

In 2020, Andy started a new venture fund of funds in the blockchain space, a venture that Adam invested in and advised. Quickly we realized that to really understand what was happening in the Web3 space, we had to do more than just invest in other Web3 funds. We also had to invest in the underlying "tokens" and projects in the space.

And that often led to a need to operate those investments—which is not what the fund of funds was set up to do. So, we created Forum3—named after that cohort we had been placed in together two decades ago—as our own operating company that would let us roll up our shirtsleeves and operate and advise actual Web3 projects, separate from what the Web3 fund was doing. After twenty years of friendship, we were in business together for the first time.

By early 2022, we had successfully (and sometimes not successfully) created, operated, and advised a half dozen Web3 projects, when we found ourselves in the board room of Starbucks founder and iconic leader Howard Schultz. He was about to start his third stint as CEO of Starbucks (this time as interim CEO) and asked if we would be willing to help bring our framework and experience to bear on what ultimately would become Starbucks Odyssey.

But soon after the launch of Odyssey, and after we played with ChatGPT and noted the emergence of a few other frontier LLMs (large language models), we started wondering aloud what this new generative AI technology would mean for how we would be helping Web3 companies, and what it meant for brands in general. And before we could even begin to answer those questions, we saw generative AI images and videos for the first time.

Within the Odyssey Discord server (the community chat platform where Starbucks Rewards members could go on an invite-only basis to share their passion, questions, and ideas for Odyssey), we saw the first amazing Starbucks fan art created with Midjourney, a generative AI platform for creating images using natural-language descriptions. This fan art looked professionally created—stunning and beautiful realistic art—but it had been generated by everyday Starbucks-loyalty members with no professional creative background. We could see how customers could become professional brand content creators without formal training of any kind. AI wouldn't just lower the barriers to normal customers being able to become professional artists, designers, coders, writers, and strategists—it would completely remove them.

Holy shit.

If generative AI could understand, learn, interact, and create text, software, images, and videos at that level today, and it was the *worst* it would ever be, then we agreed it was about to profoundly change the way brand builders ideate, produce, and implement marketing and loyalty campaigns. We felt compelled to pivot and focus on AI first, which on the one hand wasn't an easy choice, but on the other hand, we knew it wasn't really a choice at all. This was the future.

We went to work on envisioning and designing platforms and tools meant to help the leaders of brands use AI and AI-generated creative output to outperform their current processes of working, marketing, and strategic decision-making. And we committed ourselves to learn everything we could about generative AI and how it would impact brands. That led us to seeking out the smartest people we knew— ingesting every podcast and book on AI (there weren't many of the latter yet), and conversing with every AI influencer we could get to speak with us, including Sam Altman, in that transformative conversation.

. . .

The reason that AGI is so important as a concept to us, and why it left us in contemplative silence that sunny October afternoon, is because it's so disruptive and arriving so rapidly. This is why it should be so important to you, too. A five-year time estimate (give or take) for something as monumental as AGI means that it will be upon us in no time; you might have strategies that look out further than that. And whether it takes shorter or longer than that for AGI to arrive, the fact that something so disruptive, so unimaginable, is coming that quickly meant to us that we needed to do everything we could to understand how to help brands embrace and navigate this technology overall.

Thus, this book was born—to help you take those first steps to do what we ourselves are doing and feel we have no choice but to do: becoming an AI first operation. We're here to help you integrate and use AI in ways that create orders of magnitude increases in productivity and, yes, creativity, and that fundamentally change the nature of work and business. It's that big.

To do that we need to narrow the questions we're asking and the implications of their answers. Our questions can't just be about AGI itself. They can't just center on the dangers and opportunities created by a superintelligent, fully accessible, nearly free resource at the fingertips of billions of internet-connected people around the globe. It's not even about what AGI means for enterprises and entrepreneurs across general topics such as cost savings, operations, ethics, dangers, privacy, and the like. Rather, we are specifically interested in exploring what AI means for consumer-brand leaders and marketers when it comes to how they should approach strategy for brand building, marketing, and customer relationships today.

Imagine if you could test any new product idea or marketing campaign against a synthetic but perfectly predictive "community" of AI-created customers? What if the very idea of the brand creative content that you are testing came from AI itself? And the analytics, consumer insights, and plan of action could also come from AI? This isn't a random scenario plucked from some science-fiction movie. It's the type of reality that is coming soon, the essence of what we were contemplating in silence at Franklin Square park after our meeting with Sam Altman.

And that led to us wondering aloud about how this would affect customer expectations? Would customers expect a higher level of access to their favorite brands when digital access became nearly free and perfect? What about nondigital ("IRL," in real life) and digital experiences? Would one or the other become more (or less) important to consumers?

And what about the process? It won't happen overnight. But will it be reasonably steady, or start slow and then suddenly go fast? How will business leaders approach that reality and pacing?

We have called this the holy-shit moment because that is precisely what we felt in Altman's office. But an analogy to a tidal wave is apt. We know what's coming in general. And we know it's going to be powerful. But we don't know exactly when or how it will happen. To that point, when we try right now to find case studies of consumer brand marketing leaders and brand builders using AI in consumer-facing ways, we find almost no examples, save for a few fun but mostly PR-stunt experiments from Coca-Cola, Hyundai, and Heinz. Everyone has access to ChatGPT-4, Claude 2, and pi.ai. Everyone has a sense of what AI is evolving into. And yet, there's an eerie silence as business leaders look around and wonder what it will mean for them and their efforts. When will this wave hit, and how will it wash over their world?

It took about ten years from the time we understood the power of the internet, in 1999, until the social, mobile, and cloud convergent era of 2008–2010, to see the full reality and impact come to fruition. If something as impactful and transformative as AGI could possibly be upon us in half that time, what does that mean for what brands should do *now*? That's the question we now want to answer more than anything else. We aren't just pointing our company's efforts at this question, but also all of our learning and curiosity.

We're writing this book in a novel way, one that is both new and old. First, the old part: We are writing this book serially, like Dickens used to do. Dickens's motives were likely financial—magazine subscriptions shot up as readers sought the latest installment of *The Pickwick Papers*. We're more motivated by a desire to create a real-time feedback mechanism with the audience. And that leads us to the new part: This book was created not just by us but also with a community of business leaders.

Writing a book is a journey, but we were also on a parallel journey of learning about the thing we were writing about, and we wanted to share that journey with others who were as curious and dumbstruck by developments with AI as we were. So we set up a group (we called it "Our AI Journey") that would receive and react to chapters as we wrote them. Each drop was followed by a discussion with us and the group (who could also chat among themselves about AI). We had plenty of ideas about what the audience needed to know, but couldn't that be made better by asking a group of readers in real time what they needed and wanted, too?

Our editor joined many of the discussions, mostly listening for themes, ideas, and feedback to make the book stronger. We can tell you now that creating the book this way has made it both much *better* than it would have been and much *different* than it would have been. We changed our plan as we went based on the community discussions, such that the book reflects what you, the audience (by proxy of our community), were asking us for.

For example, when we asked our community of book readers what they thought our first case study should be, after they'd read the original introduction to this book, they encouraged us to step back first, and share our learning and thought journey in real time with them about this same question: What does the coming tidal wave of AI mean for them in their roles as business leaders and brand builders? They told us they needed to get a sense of the landscape before digging into the tactics of deploying AI. We listened.

So we pivoted from a straight case-study approach to something else. We said, Let's go on this journey together. Instead of case studies, per se, come with us as we interview the top thinkers and leaders in this space (at the intersection of AI, technology, and consumer brands), and comment on what they have to say to us, and to you. This is part one of the book—setting the overall landscape, understanding AI at a strategic level, from the top thinkers in the space, from Sam Altman, to Bill Gates, to Reid Hoffman, and many more. Hearing how *they* are reacting to AI (spoiler: more holy-shit moments) and framing their thinking is a great way for you to start framing yours.

With that in place, part two of the book will get tactical. We'll start to lay out how you can begin your journey to becoming an AI first operation, with early case studies of leaders who are doing it, from Sal Khan in learning to Moderna in biotech, and many others.

We believe that by the end, you'll have a good sense of where things stand, where they may be going, and what you can do *today* (what you must do today) to become AI first.

. . .

Prior to last year's breakthroughs, we thought about AI in terms either of what it was capable of now or of some esoteric future AGI that could either destroy or save civilization through its unimaginable power. It was binary thinking. But then we chatted with Sam, and we also read a paper from Google DeepMind titled "Levels of AGI for Operationalizing Progress on the Path to AGI."[1] It categorized AGI into six levels, from level 0 (no AI) to level 5 (superhuman) (see table I-1).

It also distinguished between performing a narrow set of tasks (reading X-rays, playing chess or go, etc.) and demonstrating general knowledge (wide-ranging cognitive abilities and skills). The paper got us thinking about AGI not as some line that gets crossed one day, but instead as something more like a spectrum of capabilities, something that is already here in some ways, something that's in motion, moving toward level 5 with each passing day, week, and month. The AGI we talked to Sam Altman about in October 2023 was more akin to level 4 or 5 (as capable as at least 99 percent of skilled adults across thousands of narrow professions and abilities, and/or able to outperform 100 percent of humans). This superhuman level 5 AGI is also sometimes called ASI (artificial superintelligence).

We also feel it's helpful to consider the position that some level of AGI is already here when viewed as a wider spectrum (and moving up the levels as we speak), with AGI/ASI on the horizon *moving toward us each day*. In other words, true AGI won't just be declared at a single moment in time. We will continue to see more and more "sparks of AGI" within whatever current leading frontier models we have. And that's true even now.

So, as Sam Altman said, AGI is likely going to be here in five years or so, will be coming at us in a dynamic fashion, and will affect everything, and we can't say exactly when it will arrive or precisely what it will look like. That's a lot to process. Even once you start to get your mind around it, it's hard to translate it into a plan of action or next

TABLE I-1

A leveled, matrixed approach toward classifying systems on the path to AGI based on depth (performance) and breadth (generality) of capabilities

Performance	Generality	
	Narrow	**General**
	Clearly scoped task or set of tasks	Wide range of non-physical tasks, including metacognitive tasks like learning new skills
Level 0: No AI	**Narrow Non-AI**	**General Non-AI**
	Calculator software; compiler	Human-in-the-loop computing, e.g., Amazon Mechanical Turk
Level 1: Emerging Equal to or some-what better than an unskilled human	**Emerging Narrow AI** GOFAI (Boden, 2014); simple rule-based systems, e.g., SHRDLU (Winograd, 1971)	**Emerging AGI** ChatGPT (OpenAI, 2023), Bard (Anil et al., 2023), Llama 2 (Touvron et al., 2023), Gemini (Pichai and Hassabis, 2023)
Level 2: Competent At least 50th percentile of skilled adults	**Competent Narrow AI** Toxicity detectors such as Jigsaw (Das et al., 2022); Smart Speakers such as Siri (Apple), Alexa (Amazon), or Google Assistant (Google); VQA systems such as PaLI (Chen et al., 2023); Watson (IBM); SOTA LLMs for a subset of tasks (e.g., short essay writing, simple coding)	**Competent AGI** Not yet achieved
Level 3: Expert At least 90th percentile of skilled adults	**Expert Narrow AI** Spelling and grammar checkers such as Grammarly (Grammarly, 2023); generative image models such as Imagen (Saharia et al., 2022) or Dall-E 2 (Ramesh et al., 2022)	**Expert AGI** Not yet achieved
Level 4: Virtuoso At least 99th percentile of skilled adults	**Virtuoso Narrow AI** Deep Blue (Campbell et al., 2002), AlphaGo (Silver et al., 2016; 2017)	**Virtuoso AGI** Not yet achieved
Level 5: Superhuman Outperforms 100% of humans	**Superhuman Narrow AI** AlphaFold (Jumper et al., 2021; Varadi et al., 2021), AlphaZero (Silver et al., 2018), StockFish (Stockfish, 2023)	**Artificial Superintelligence (ASI)** Not yet achieved

Source: Meredith Ringel Morris et al., "Position: Levels of AGI for Operationalizing Progress on the Path to AGI," *Proceedings of the International Conference on Machine Learning*, no. 235 (2024), doi.org/10.48550/arXiv.2311.02462.

steps today. When we processed this, we could see why our community was thinking, *Whoa, back up. First, help me understand.*

At the risk of oversimplifying how to translate this into action, we see three possible next steps for you:

- **Be a deer in headlights.** Don't do anything with AI, because soon enough AGI will be able to do anything we can possibly think of in terms of services, technology, or knowledge transfer.

- **Look for efficiency.** Think about the current AI capabilities and try to do the things you've been trained to do to help the business increase productivity, reduce overhead, and so forth.

- **Experiment and learn.** Start using the latest AI tools in your work now to experiment, learn, and practice how to operate in the coming age of AGI.

Option one is off the table. You lose if you go that way. Examples of letting things come to you and paying a dear price for doing so are legion and become legends of disruption. Here's just one recent example: In April 2021, Apple rolled out iOS 14.5, which allowed users to opt out of publishers and advertisers being able to use their data for targeted digital advertising. A full 75 percent of consumers opted out. By February 2023, Facebook said this change accounted for a $10 billion drop in its business. Marketers who hadn't anticipated this discovered that it became much more difficult to acquire customers using what had become almost everyone's default playbook of just specifying a target customer and budgeting digital ad dollars.

Option two is table stakes.

Option three is where we choose to focus our exploration with you. We believe it's the most effective approach, and it's not just gut instinct that tells us that. It turns out these options weren't much different during the last great disruption: the advent of the internet. We can look at examples from Web1 and Web2 companies that took option 3 and how it served them well.

With the original Web1 dot-com boom—and despite the hype and bust—those companies that understood in 1999 that every business and person on this planet would use the web in their daily life (and as a foundational fabric for their productivity) were advantaged. This was because that framework led them to be fast to experiment and learn how their business might look when everyone was online, well before that was the case. Broadband connectivity for all and ubiquitous mobile computing (smartphones and tablets) were still nearly a decade away, but the winning companies were ones that were the first to *act as if it was already the reality.*

A great example of this is Dell Computers. As the internet era emerged in the late '90s, Dell immediately set up an e-commerce channel, practically invented the concept of omnichannel retailing, and printed Dell.com on all of its boxes and computers when that was still exceedingly rare and probably looked odd to the world. By imagining what its business would look like in a world of ubiquitous connection, it learned faster than its competitors and it dominated the retail computer-sales market from 1998 to 2008, going from $12 billion in revenues in 1998 to $60 billion in 2008, a 500 percent increase in a decade, unheard of at that time for a $12 billion company. Apple grew more in that time but started the decade with half the revenue of Dell and ended it still $23 billion behind Dell (from $6 billion to $37 billion).

As the 2000s progressed, Netflix and Spotify were option 3 companies. They each started before mobile and ubiquitous broadband, but ultimately thrived and became category leaders because the landscape evolved as they predicted. Netflix thought of itself as offering on-demand streaming video, with personalization and original content, none of which was possible before the last convergent era of ubiquitous mobile broadband computing devices (smartphones). Spotify was founded on the idea of free, on-demand music streaming (ad supported with freemium paid model) in 2006, *before* the iPhone came out, and long before smartphones were ubiquitous. Both companies built business models that only really worked when the dot on the horizon became a reality.

Starbucks is another example. The Starbucks mobile-payment, mobile-loyalty, and mobile-ordering platform follows much the same playbook: imagining what the world will be like in a year or two—where the proverbial puck is going—and experimenting well ahead of that. Starbucks offered this new thing called "mobile payment" long before Apple Pay and Google Pay. "All you will need is your phone, and you can forget your wallet at home." And same with mobile loyalty and mobile ordering. Starbucks acted as if everyone had smartphones and couldn't live without them long before that was true. But that didn't stop the company from experimenting and incorporating the mobile tech and being a pioneer for each feature, and it now has an industry-leading platform vital to the company's success.

We are keen on the idea of companies (starting with our own) creating strategies and services that will only be *more* effective when access to level 4 and level 5 AGI becomes ubiquitous. Even though, as Sam Altman himself told us, it's not possible to truly know what the world will look like when that happens, it's highly likely (dare we say, almost certain) that life will go on, and brands will continue to make products and serve customers. Marketing campaigns will still need to be created and implemented. Commerce will still need to be fulfilled.

Business leaders can emulate that future right now, with AI still in its current level 1 or level 2 status. That's because the current frontier LLM models are already capable of more than you think, and the combination of humans and AI can create much of what true AGI might look like. You can already set up your own custom GPT for free, or even train your own model if you are a large company—and then put the tools into the hands of your company and your customers in a way that will not only create efficiencies but also advance your product/service experiences. And if you do that now, imagine how well positioned you will be over the next five years as the underlying AI moves up the AGI spectrum levels.

It's a lot, we know. We still have days that make us freeze and say it again, "Holy shit." But you can become AI first. We're starting to see companies that are emulating the Dells and Starbucks and Spotifys of the past disruptions. We'll share the stories of many of them with you on this journey.

Let's start, now.

Part One

WHAT IS HAPPENING?

Chapter 1

HUMAN + MACHINE

About two months after Sam Altman blew our minds, they were blown again. This time by Reid Hoffman, who greeted us for our meeting with him by saying, "Sorry to keep you waiting. I was just speaking to the Pope and his team at the Vatican, helping them shape their thoughts on AI."[1] It was early December 2023, and this time we were in the lobby of a top venture-capital firm, Greylock Partners, doing a double take at what we had just heard.

Hoffman explained to us what he told the team at the Vatican. He had been urging them to stop focusing only on the headlines about how AI had the potential someday to turn on humanity like the Terminator, and instead to focus on the ways that AI—*today*—could actually help humanity. "For example," he said to us, "if the six billion people on this planet that don't have access to a general-practitioner doctor could suddenly use their smartphones to use ChatGPT-4 or Pi [a

ChatGPT-like AI system from Inflection AI] to get reasonably good, instant, free medical help, then that was a good thing, a transformatively good thing, and something that the Pope and his team should care about."

It was a simple example of a theme that would come up again and again in our conversation with Hoffman: human + machine. So much ink has been spilled pitting AI against humanity. Here was someone thinking about how the two might—and likely will—work together, which is exactly what we'd been thinking about when it comes to how business leaders should approach this amazing new technology.

In this example, humans, using a machine (AI via smartphone), could change the face of health care, and it was going to take shape over the next two to four years. It was a theme that would permeate the next sixty minutes, which felt like five minutes.

. . .

Reid Hoffman has a rich and varied entrepreneurial and technology-focused background and an incredible track record. He was not only part of the "PayPal mafia" as the former COO of that company but went on to be the founder and CEO of LinkedIn, and a general partner at Greylock Partners. He's now on the board of Microsoft (which bought LinkedIn), and crucial to our conversation with you, he was one of the founding supporters of OpenAI, along with Sam Altman and Elon Musk. He is also a cofounder of one of the top foundational large language model (LLM) AI companies—Inflection AI—along with DeepMind cofounder Mustafa Suleyman.

He is as involved in, and knows as much about, the impact of generative AI and LLMs as anyone on the planet—especially as they relate to the intersection of AI with company building, organizational design, and marketing workflow.

We explained our own AI journey to Hoffman. We told him how we had started building a company focusing on helping brands embrace, navigate, and leverage generative AI to fuel their own strategic growth objectives, and that we were writing a serialized book with Harvard Business Review Press to share our journey and our learnings.

Hoffman smiled. Sitting on the conference-room table in front of him, next to his laptop, were two copies of an orange-colored hardcover book. He picked them up and handed us each one of the books on the spot. It turns out that Hoffman had written a book in the last year on his own journey around his use of OpenAI's ChatGPT-4 ("GPT-4").[2] It was titled *Impromptu: Amplifying Our Humanity Through AI*, and it was written with a coauthor, GPT-4. As he handed us each a copy, he signed the book: "Shared projects!—Reid."

"I'm happy to share my thoughts with you both, and have you include them in your book," Hoffman said, as we casually flipped through his book.

In less than ten minutes we all realized that we had a shared passion and a mutual interest in figuring this all out and sharing our learnings with others. We dove in.

A quick glance at Hoffman's book indicated that this was about to be a great meeting.

As one of OpenAI's founders, Hoffman had access to GPT-4 prior to its public release, in March 2023. In fact, he had access to GPT-4 prior even to the public release of GPT-3.5, in November 2022, the release that sent shockwaves through the world and kicked off the modern generative AI era and craze.

In the introduction to his book, Hoffman started journaling his first impressions of generative AI and what these new foundational LLMs were capable of. "It seemed clear to me that GPT-4 had reached a new level of proficiency compared to its predecessors," Hoffman wrote, "So while GPT-4 wasn't a new device per se, it felt to me to be something that could become as indispensable as our smartphones—a 12-in-1 multi-tool for your brain."

"Much of what we do as modern people—at work and beyond—is to process information and generate action. GPT-4 will massively speed your ability to do these things, and with greater breadth and scope," the book continued. "If you simply let GPT-4 do all the work, with no human oversight or engagement, it's a less powerful tool. But when human users treat GPT-4 as a copilot or a collaborative partner, it becomes far more powerful. You compound GPT-4's computational generativity, efficiency, synthetic powers, and capacity to scale with human creativity, human judgment, and human guidance."

There it was again: human + machine.

We wanted to start our conversation with Hoffman right where we left off with Sam Altman, feeling inspired (and a little awestruck) by the concept that these models were going to improve so quickly, and that an artificial general intelligence (i.e., AGI)–like reality was something that all businesses would have to embrace and navigate. So now we needed to know: What did that look like? How should businesses prepare for that? How could an understanding of this soon-to-be-reality be leveraged as an advantage in a competitive marketplace? Specifically, could brand builders and marketers use this technology in a new way to help their companies grow?

So, our first questions to Hoffman focused on his thoughts on AGI, staying in the thought zone of "Where is the puck going?"

Hoffman didn't hesitate to answer what an AGI world would look like over the next three to seven years, his estimate for the time frame involved.

He said there are two ways to think about it; two "poles" of framing it up, as he put it.

On the one hand, he suggested, you can think of AGI as being achieved when the AI is essentially capable of doing a massive set of cognitive tasks that used to be doable only by human beings. People would then use this AGI as a copilot for almost every cognitive task or problem they are solving, and this copilot factor in the workplace would have an overall five-to-ten-times multiplier effect on the speed and capability of thought and output. Hoffman noted that we are nearly there now, but the reason you wouldn't yet say we are at an AGI state based on this framework is because GPT-4 can't quite plan out fifteen steps, as opposed to five steps, for example. This more capable iteration of AGI will be realized in the next three to seven years, for the most part, he suggested.

The second "pole" of framing up AGI, he continued, will be achieved when the AI has some sort of agency and humanlike general capability and when it will be designed to act and learn on its own to accomplish a lot of goals without too much human assistance. Hoffman suggested this is more of how Altman thinks of AGI. Hoffman commented that this definition of AGI is more confusing, insofar as it's hard to imagine what it would mean for how individual humans and businesses would conduct themselves, and anyway is likely farther out than five years.

We focused in on the first pole. "At minimum, every task that involves language will have a copilot," he said. "If you are using language at all in the running of your business, you will use an AI copilot for the enterprise. And this will apply to every single industry. For example, if someone says, wait, I'm in the steel-manufacturing indus-try, and that doesn't apply to me, right? The answer is: yes, it does. Even if the use of an AI copilot doesn't invent a new method of steel manufacturing, the steel company still does sales, marketing, and business analysis. Those all involve language. The use of an always on AI copilot will still have a big impact on all of those areas."

We then asked, What does working with an AI copilot look like in practice?

Hoffman surmised that if each functional leader is using AI con-tinually to help them plan, analyze, strategize, and articulate, it will be like having a "10X multiplier" on every key function in your com-pany. He didn't say if that meant 10X on output or quality, but we know that "10X" is a term thrown around in Silicon Valley—for exam-ple, a "10X engineer"—and refers to a combination of speed and qual-ity upgrade from the average.

Then the topic turned to what this meant for resource planning. "If you suddenly have a 10X multiplier on the sales force, does that mean you don't have salespeople?" he asked rhetorically. "No, you still need salespeople. But the workflow may be very different, because—for example—processes around how leads are identified and qualified, using AI agents to help filter prospects, etc., will all still come into play but be greatly AI-assisted." The point is that companies will still care about the sales function just as deeply.

"Same with marketing," Hoffman continued. "Even in an AGI-reality world, businesses still will compete with one another. In that future, what will my marketing department look like? You will prob-ably still spend the same amount of money marketing, because you still need to play the market-share game—but you will have a new set of tools. As opposed to having ten people doing form entry, you will have less, maybe zero to one person. But the need for humans to work with AI is where the amplification really happens."

Hoffman surmised that this concept of an enterprise copilot would be de rigueur in the near future. It's the human-plus-machine concept that was coming into focus for us. There are twenty years' worth of books and articles written about this notion of human + machine—including a recent book from Harvard Business Review Press titled, literally, *Human + Machine*. There's no term of art for this yet. In fact, Hoffman talked about how the current term for it is *centaur* (as in, half human, half horse—but instead it's half human, half AI). We agreed that's probably not the best term to describe the notion. The concept we at Forum3 had been bouncing around is how it's sort of like a human in an AI "mech suit" (think, Iron Man's machine that Robert Downey Jr. steps into)—but we all agreed, while chuckling out loud, that that wasn't any better a term than *centaur*.

Hoffman suggested that the concept of how much leverage you can get with human + machine is to think of what the steam engine did for the Industrial Revolution. He said, "AI is like the steam engine for the mind." By the early 1800s, steam-powered machines allowed entire factories and industries to be much more productive, and freed up humans to focus on more-creative aspects of company and industry building. You still needed humans to direct the endeavor, but the new paradigm of human + steam–powered machines became the norm for any industrious company looking to truly grow and compete in that new era.

Enterprise AI copilots are this era's version of the steam engine.

We also spent quite a bit of time talking about AI agents, the term for software that has the power and intelligence of AI but that also has the ability to act independently and autonomously. The idea is that you give an AI agent a goal and write code that not only allows it to have access to the underlying AI intelligence but that also allows it to sense its environment, interact with its environment, take actions, learn, and achieve its programmed goals. This is different from the helpful-assistant model for an AI system like ChatGPT today, a model that is simply reactive and nonautonomous, requiring you to input a prompt before the AI can give you an answer.

Here is an example of the difference between the current capabilities of a multimodal LLM without an agent and one with an agent. Today, you can ask ChatGPT-4 to help you construct an itinerary for an upcoming trip to Disneyland with your family. You could give it context, explain your preferences, and ask it to come up with a full step-by-step itinerary for your trip, and it will do so beautifully. But it can't yet book any of the elements of your trip for you. It can only give you the recipe and details for how to plan the trip. An agent would actually be able to follow the recipe and buy the right flight tickets, including payment details and mileage-plan details; book the hotel room; reserve the rental car; buy the park tickets; and make the dinner reservations. Of course, you would have to authenticate and connect the agent to your credit card, your loyalty program, and your travel preferences, but an agent would be able to take these actions for you, including perhaps having chats and conversations with the various booking systems and support staff.

In the new AI era, Hoffman said, "we will have to get comfortable living in an AI agent universe, where there are tons of AI agents everywhere. There will be multiple AI agents for each enterprise. Both internal-facing agents and external agents."

Standalone AI agents programmed with a specific task and specific goals, and armed with full AI capabilities, could and would transform entire industries in an AGI era. Think, for example, of self-driving cars that are powered by AI agents with a single overriding goal: get people and cargo from point A to point B, and without harming any-one or damaging anything in the process. Hoffman cited the statistic that forty thousand people die every year in transportation accidents. "People make mistakes and do dumb things," he noted, "like getting drunk or texting while driving. It might be smart to get humans out of the process of driving."

It's worth noting here why we don't see a lot of (or almost any) AI agents in the wild right now. AI can make mistakes. We've seen exam-ples of factual mistakes from LLMs (called hallucinations), where the AI will literally just make up facts or sources for answers it gives. Plus, AI has been seen struggling from time to time with math equations and sometimes even basic logic. Given these limitations, you can imagine why it's taking time to develop AI agent systems, and why it will take time for everyday people and companies to trust these agents with important data, financial access, and anything that involves life-threatening consequences.

That being said, there is a ton of capital and energy going into the development of AI agent tools right now. So it's understandable why Hoffman is focused on how agents will be a part of our AI-infused near future. On the specific topic of AI agents in the corporate con-text, he mentioned that we should think both about external-facing agents—like those doing customer service/support or taking orders—and internal-facing agents. With regard to the latter, Hoffman said we should get Microsoft CEO Satya Nadella to demonstrate the latest ver-sion of Microsoft Teams, to show us how it is already able to incorpo-rate internal agents that sit in on virtual Teams meetings and that can take notes, identify people that weren't in the meeting that should be briefed, track follow-up action items, and provide links to information resources within the company. All companies have work done in teams, and this is a great example of how an internal AI agent might just sit in on every company meeting in the future, as a member of the team, with specific administrative goals and capabilities.

. . .

The conversation turned to whether AI agents can actually transform certain functions. For example, can agents transform customer service into account management and sales as well? This would create entirely new job roles, for both the AI agents and for the humans programming and directing those agents. For example, imagine that when you contacted an LLM-powered chat agent for customer support, the agent was instructed to look for signs of an opportunity (using its newfound LLM-based powers of persuasion) to sell you a new product or service, or convince you to upgrade to a premium feature. This is much harder for a non-LLM-based AI agent to accomplish given its lack of dynamic understanding and language capabilities.

Hovering over this conversation—and over your thinking on AI, we're sure—is that ubiquitous, lowering sense that it will kill jobs, period. But we weren't arriving at that point of view in our chat. Some jobs will be replaced, yes, but many more will be created. New skills will be needed. Buggy-whip manufacturers went out of business when cars came along, sure, but then there were drivetrain engineers, car washes, and windshield-wiper manufacturers who sprang into existence. Likewise, AI creates a new type of skill and job—while removing some jobs and changing others. An example is creatives. Today, a graphic designer has to be a great visual thinker *and* have fine motor skills to translate that through the design tool (for instance, Photoshop). With AI tools and agents, what will really matter won't be fine motor control but just visual thinking, Hoffman postulated. "The tools may be changing," he said, "but the visual thinking and creative directing matters as much as or more than ever."

As it was getting close to the time to wrap up, we moved the meeting from the topic of AGI and the next three to seven years to inquire about the here and now. We asked, "What concrete advice would you have for business leaders for what to do today?"

"Start experimenting and playing with this AI as copilot now, as in *right now*," he said, with emphasis. "Maybe even start using some agents in your workflow if you can find someone to develop them for you." Starting now is as much about developing in business leaders the mental flexibility they need to figure out "How does this apply to me and my business?" Only business leaders can connect those dots for their enterprise and field.

Moreover, he said, "start thinking about your 'offense game' and your 'defense game' using these tools. Your offense game is figuring out where might the incorporation of generative AI to your workflow allow you to do something that would give you market share, margin, differentiation by using this. Your experimentation should inform this. Does this change my positioning? Should I change my product offering? My marketing?"

On the defense side, think about what your competition might be doing with these AI tools. And this also helps inform the offense thinking. And so on.

. . .

From our perspective, the discussion with Hoffman was incredibly helpful and specific.

First off, we were offered a specific vision and solution for how to think about what a new workflow for business leaders might look like in an advanced AI future. That road map starts with immediately experimenting and becoming proficient with AI copiloting at the functional leadership and strategy level, imagining what your competitors might be doing in this vein with AI, and possibly even imagining how AI agents can help be transformational or innovative in your company.

Second, the discussion with Hoffman immediately conjured up parallels in our minds with the last major digital-transformation era: social, mobile, and cloud.

The opening up of the iPhone App Store in 2008 began the most recent technological convergence era, often referred to as the social, mobile, cloud era. Around the same time that the iPhone App Store opened (with Android not far behind), a relatively new company called Facebook was also taking off, creating the social media phenomenon. And both of those momentous things happened against the backdrop of cloud-computing capabilities becoming ubiquitous thanks to Amazon Web Services (AWS), Azure, and Google Cloud.

That particular convergence of new technologies went on to disrupt and change the landscape around every aspect of society and business, and that was particularly true of brand marketing and customer engagement. Every major brand developed a social media, mobile-app, and data-driven marketing approach. And, the convergence gave extra importance to organizational and strategic thinking in the general area of digital transformation, creating such work titles at consumer brands as chief digital officer and chief experience officer.

By the time the pandemic hit, every consumer brand in the world had spent the twelve years between 2008 and 2020 migrating to a digital-first mentality, particularly as it related to their customer-acquisition strategy and engagement tactics. Targeting customers based on their previous clicks and searches, or on how certain customers looked like other customers based on social media engagement or search data, all led to a clear digital-marketing playbook for growing your brand. Paid digital advertising, using data-driven targeting and programmatic delivery, particularly on social media and search platforms, became table stakes. And it dominated the playbook for marketing and growth.

Similarly, seemingly every consumer brand came up with a mobile strategy, a mobile app, a points-based loyalty scheme, and a digital-delivery plan where possible. Digital-engagement and -convenience features became the norm, not the exception.

About four years into the social, mobile, and cloud convergent era, it seemed like something clicked in the minds of every business leader. They all understood that they needed a digital strategy and maybe even a chief digital officer (or the like), but they were always a little confused around the paradigm or rubric for how to implement this kind of a transformation in their own particular organization. But once they had their aha moment around digital, the question "How can we use digital to accelerate this or improve that?" permeated nearly every conversation in the workplace.

But the tricky part back then—just as it is now with generative AI—was, How do you connect these dots in the right way? In the preceding digital-transformation era, it required people in the organization who could see the Venn diagram encompassing the core business issues, the power of digital, and how to blend the power of both in the right way. It was one part science, one part art, and one part architecture.

A great example of this, in the heart of that last convergent era, is how Starbucks tackled the challenge of digital transformation. In 2008, in the middle of the great financial recession, Howard Schultz had just come back as CEO for the second time. He was leading and masterminding a broader transformational agenda for the company (well chronicled in his bestselling book, *Onward*). And as part of that broader agenda, he had a sense that the company could and should be incorporating digital innovation as a customer-experience enhancement and competitive advantage.

So Howard and the leadership team at Starbucks embraced a totally new organizational concept and position called the chief digital officer, with responsibilities ranging from strategy to technology to marketing to something completely new. The company would create a team and a mandate around the broader strategic belief that its customers were becoming more and more digitally savvy and using mobile phones in their everyday lives. Connecting the dots on the exact strategy would be for the digital team to discover, architect, evangelize, and implement. And it would have to be done in a matrixed and integrated way. You obviously couldn't just bolt a digital strategy onto twenty thousand coffee stores and billions of cups of coffee being served each year.

The chief digital officer was as much a strategy as it was a person or a team.

For starters, it required buy-in from top leaders—usually including the CEO—for a nontraditional approach to organizational design and strategy. Instead of the usual functional boundaries between marketing, technology, strategy, and operations, it required allowing for a blending of these functions in new ways. It meant taking a bottom-up, connect-the-dots approach to figuring out how digital platforms, tools, and experiences could integrate and enhance the customer experience and relationship at the company. It took early experimentation and early learnings to flesh out how it might best come into shape.

The results of this approach worked.

In 2010, Starbucks launched one-click free Wi-Fi in all of its company-owned stores based in the United States. Around the same time, the company launched a point-based loyalty program, tied to its payment (gift) card program. Shortly thereafter, Starbucks launched an iOS mobile app connected to both its loyalty program and its payment (gift) card programs.

By 2013, the company had the leading loyalty and mobile-payment program in the world. In 2014, Starbucks piloted "mobile order ahead" on the app, tied to its loyalty program, as well as to its payment card— "Mobile Order and Pay," they called it. By 2016 it was one of the most successful digital ecosystems of any brand in the world.

Today, more than 60 percent of all transactions in the United States are via this mobile/loyalty ecosystem, with nearly half of those transactions being order-ahead transactions. Starbucks currently has over 75 million active loyalty members globally, with over 33 million in the United States alone.

You can imagine a chief AI officer position taking a similar trajectory for companies today (and you will learn about one such company in a later chapter, a biotech company). The AI era is coming around the corner, if it's not here already. The parallels are obvious, even if the exact path for each company is not.

. . .

Hearing Hoffman's vision of a future dominated by AI copilots and AI agents—a vision we fully subscribe to—we realized we were in a situation similar to the preceding transformational era. We started asking ourselves the obvious next question: How will business organizations and leaders go from 0 to 1 in this area, understanding the power of generative AI and connecting the dots between their own key decision-making processes and this new technology?

As we left that meeting, we realized that our own AI journey and this book project were clearly taking on a pattern, and one that we were eager to continue. Through a combination of factors, we had now found ourselves in the amazing position of having access to the top AI leaders and thinkers in the world, all of whom have a lot to say about where AI is going and how it is going to change the shape of the world in general; and how it is certainly going to change the face of how business leaders will make decisions and build their companies.

Our journey was taking shape. We realized that we needed now to explore more around the question of how organizations and leaders will go about adopting this new technology and leveraging it. How will they have their own aha moments like Hoffman did when he first got access to GPT-4, as he documented in his book? How will they develop this new muscle, and implement their own version of an AI-based transformational agenda?

These questions are pulling us organically to the next chapter in our AI journey.

Chapter 2

PRODUCTIVITY REDEFINED

I n the early 1970s, in a modest office nestled within Xerox PARC in Palo Alto, California, a young Bill Gates experienced a revelation that would chart the course of his life and, unknowingly, the trajectory of the modern world. There, in the heart of Silicon Valley's unassuming innovation hub, stood the Xerox Alto. The Alto, a large workstation from the 1970s, is largely considered to be the first personal computer ever created. It featured a graphical user interface (GUI), a mouse, Ethernet networking, and the ability to run multiple applications simultaneously. It was one of the first computers to use a WYSIWYG (What You See Is What You Get) text editor. While the Alto did not succeed commercially, it nevertheless had a significant influence on the development of future computer systems. For young Bill Gates, the Alto wasn't just a computer, it was a portal to the future; a vision of what computers could become. For Gates, the Alto was a revolution waiting to happen.

Years later, we found ourselves interviewing Bill Gates as part of our AI-journey book project. In contrast to the Bill Gates who visited PARC in the 1970s, this Bill Gates not only had a gray hair or two but was now one of the most accomplished and experienced technologists and business leaders in the history of the world. He had taken his vision for the future of computing and made it a reality. His company, Microsoft, has become one of the most valuable and respected companies, not just in the technology industry but in any industry. And the Bill and Melinda Gates Foundation has donated over $50 billion to causes such as eradicating diseases, preventing destructive climate change, and furthering education around the globe.

But in terms of energy, curiosity, intelligence, and articulation, you wouldn't see any difference between the younger Gates and the one we found in front of us during the interview.

As Gates reflected on that day at Xerox, his eyes lit up with the same fervor and excitement that he felt back then and that he felt more recently when Sam Altman showed him OpenAI's ChatGPT. "Seeing ChatGPT ace an AP biology exam, with explanatory comments showing it was grasping the concepts involved, was like standing at the precipice of a whole new world," Gates mused, "similar to my first encounter with the Alto."[1] Gates recalled the Alto's graphical interface—a stark departure from the esoteric command lines that dominated computing at the time. Because the Alto used an intuitive GUI interface, in which you pointed and clicked, it was a machine that spoke the user's language, much like how today's AI converses, learns, and even jokes in natural human vernacular. "Back then," Gates continued, "it was about making computers personal and intuitive. Today, AI is set to make them even more so—insightful, adaptive, and perhaps eventually, truly intelligent."

Gates told us the story of seeing the Alto and how it inspired the vision for Microsoft's early dominance as a computer company, which included the vision of a computer on every desktop and the development of Windows, Office, and various other Microsoft products. That vision would take Microsoft more than ten years, but it indeed came to life, and it would be hard to top. But Gates wondered aloud if seeing ChatGPT perform its magic wasn't a more significant and inspiring moment even than the Alto moment was approximately fifty years earlier. As he wondered about this possibility, he was reflective, wistful, and excited. What if it were true—what if this AI moment really was more significant for Gates than when he saw the Alto?

Once again, we couldn't help but wonder generally about AI's implications for the everyday world we lived in, and for brands and marketers more specifically? If seeing ChatGPT for the first time is a more significant indicator for Gates of the future than Gates seeing the Alto back in the '70s, then it would seem to back up what Sam Altman said about how, at some point in the next five to ten years, we would likely see 95 percent of today's marketing and creative work be impacted in terms of speed, cost, and capability via artificial general intelligence–like tools in the hands of almost anyone. Watching Gates tell us this story and make this connection was yet another holy-shit moment in our AI journey that wasn't lost on us.

. . .

We began our conversation with Gates by catching him up on our conversations with Sam Altman and Reid Hoffman, specifically around their thoughts on AGI, enterprise copilots, and agents. We asked him generally what he saw as the likely impact of AI on business workflow over the next few years. "There are some big scenarios, like coding, sales, support, and data analytics—each of which are significant job categories, particularly for big companies," Gates began. "The copilot capability within those areas will be creating significant productivity increases. Microsoft has seen that in its support cases. We've seen that in our programmers. We see that in our data-analytics stuff. Obviously, we get the internal versions early, but this stuff is improving pretty dramatically." In just the one-year period since ChatGPT had been widely available, and in which Microsoft had incorporated many of ChatGPT's capabilities into its offerings through a variety of copilot features, certain business functions had already begun regularly leveraging these tools with immediate and sometimes eye-popping effects on productivity. In fact, on a podcast that Gates had recently recorded with Sam Altman, Gates said that software developers were seeing up to a 300 percent productivity improvement by using the code-writing copilot capabilities.

As our discussion with Gates meandered through the corridors of AI's potential generally, we lasered in on this fundamental question surrounding AI: What does productivity entail in the age of AI? And we wondered, what would it mean for brands and marketing? Would it just be a cost-savings exercise, or could it somehow also improve the actual creative work and its effectiveness? For Gates, the answer was clearly that it could do both. "Productivity," he said, "isn't a mere measure of output per hour; it's about enhancing the quality and creativity of our achievements."

Gates leaned forward, his eyes lighting up as he broke down productivity into a sort of mathematical formula, as he sometimes does. "Productivity, in its essence, is a function of three variables: quantity, quality, and efficiency," he said. "It's about doing more, doing better, or doing it with less." Gates drew parallels to the evolution of newspapers in the digital era, a sector transformed by the advent of computers. "Before digital typesetting, newspaper layouts were arduous, manual tasks. Computers didn't just speed up this process; they enriched the quality of content. With computers, journalists had more time to focus on their stories, layouts became more engaging, and the overall quality of newspapers soared. That's the real essence of productivity." Even with computers, newspapers still only published physical newspapers one time per day, but they allowed for digital publishing and 24/7 updates. For newspapers, productivity increase was represented by an increase in quality reporting, as well as innovation around the medium itself.

It's worth unpacking the point Gates was getting at here with respect to the relationship between productivity and quality. Everyone knows that a boost in productivity will allow you either to produce more of something in the same amount of time or to produce the same amount of something in a faster period of time. In other words, a boost in productivity equals more or faster output—or the same output with fewer resources required to get there. That part is obvious. But what's less obvious is what happens when you get a boost in productivity, but you have no need to produce something in either greater quantities or in a faster time frame. The ability to optimize/reallocate resources in this scenario may give you a boost in *qualitative* output. If I'm able to finish quicker or put fewer human resources into producing something, it frees up my time and resources to do a better job at the one thing I'm producing in a given time frame. In this way, while AI is clearly a productivity-enhancing tool, it has the immediate potential to also be a quality-enhancing tool for knowledge workers. Better research, better decisions, better insights—those are examples of what AI could unlock if you take this framework to its natural conclusion.

What does this advancement mean for brands and marketers? At Forum3, we guide marketing teams toward adopting an AI first approach to tap into significant productivity enhancements. Adopting an AI first strategy in marketing not only amplifies productivity but also ushers in unprecedented cost efficiency and creative agility. A primary application area for marketers embarking on this journey is content creation. Large language models (LLMs), with their prowess in crafting compelling blog posts, headlines, and holistic content strategies, serve as foundational blocks. These AI models adeptly chart out content calendars, brainstorm article ideas, and seamlessly transition from ideation to execution, transforming marketers from primary content creators to strategic editors. Specialized tools like Jasper, Copy.ai, and Canva are at the forefront of this innovation, specializing in streamlining these marketing tasks.

Moreover, AI's influence extends beyond digital content to revolutionize traditional marketing mediums such as photo shoots. By employing AI for background generation, brands can simulate lavish settings without the hefty price tag associated with location shoots. This approach not only reduces costs but also enhances the productivity of content creation across mediums.

The burgeoning domain of video marketing is another arena where AI's impact is palpable, with companies like Veed.io and Remini.ai doing interesting things. With platforms like Wistia introducing an array of AI tools, from auto transcripts to AI-powered video highlights, marketers are now equipped to produce more-engaging and -personalized content faster than ever. Notably, Spotify's integration of AI to customize playlists and Wistia's AI tools for video marketing exemplify the tangible benefits of AI in enhancing user engagement and streamlining content strategies.

There are a few other examples that illustrate the power of AI in brands and customer experiences. In the realm of e-commerce, Shopify has introduced AI-powered features such as Shopify Magic, streamlining store management tasks from marketing to customer support, underscoring the transformative potential of AI in enhancing customer experiences and operational efficiency. Duolingo's integration of AI, particularly through Duolingo Max, exemplifies AI's role in personalized education, offering adaptive learning experiences that cater to individual strengths and weaknesses.

In this new era, where AI-driven marketing strategies are becoming the norm, brands that harness these technologies to foster a more interactive and personalized relationship with their consumers will not only achieve greater efficiency and creativity but also set a new benchmark for customer engagement and brand loyalty.

Beyond new qualitative improvement and new forms of creativity that AI's efficiency can engender, there's another, possibly more exciting AI effect. To explain, Gates turned to health care. "In health care," he said, "AI's role transcends the boundaries of traditional productivity metrics. It's not just about diagnosing patients faster. AI is unveiling insights previously out of reach to humans, identifying subtleties in medical images that even seasoned professionals might miss." It was as unobvious as the productivity-can-equal-quality idea, but once you saw it, you got excited. What if the AI *sees* patterns, insights, conclusions that are too hard for humans to get at? That's a form of productivity, yes—but it's like an "unlock" mechanism, allowing for something to be possible in a time frame, with a given amount of resources, that was previously not possible. Is this the same quality improvement mentioned above? Not exactly. It's a change in what is even possible.

When thinking about this insight from the marketer's lens, it means AI is going to be able to identify market segments that humans can't see, or that humans miss. AI will assist in channel mix as well as in value-prop development. "It's no longer about shooting arrows in the dark," Gates said. "AI is enabling marketers to craft campaigns that resonate on a deeper, more personal level with consumers. By analyzing vast data sets, AI helps understand consumer behavior, predict trends, and tailor messages that strike a chord."

In the marketing domain, two companies that are enabling the shift to AI first marketing are Adobe and Mailchimp. Adobe, notably, is doing so through Adobe Sensei GenAI and Adobe Firefly, showcasing AI's impact on creativity, enabling creators to generate images, text effects, and color palettes from simple text prompts, thereby revolutionizing the creative process. Mailchimp, by including predictive segmentation and an AI-enhanced email content generator, is showing how AI can refine email marketing strategies, making them more effective and personalized. These are just two of the many companies that stand to use generative AI to transform marketing as we know it.

Around the same time as the conversation with Gates, coincidentally, Harvard Business School (with assistance from Wharton School Professor Ethan Mollick) published a fascinating study with Boston Consulting Group (BCG) on productivity in the AI era.[2] The study, a comprehensive examination of generative AI's impact on business, reveals how AI is reshaping organizational functions and processes in knowledge-intensive domains. Significantly, it includes a striking insight: the advent of AI won't be an incremental change but a sudden and fundamental shift in how businesses are able to increase both the speed and the quality of their decision-making.

The study's experiments, conducted in collaboration with BCG, involved three phases, including demographic profiling, task completions, and interviews. Two distinct tasks were tested: one within AI's capabilities and another outside its bounds. The results demonstrated significant productivity and quality gains in tasks where AI was applicable.

The study found that deploying generative AI tools across enterprises can yield broad productivity gains of up to 25 percent, along with qualitative improvements of a whopping 40 percent. (See figure 2-1.) These gains align with Gates's concept of doing more and better with less, as AI tools enhance both the quantity and the quality of output. The Harvard/BCG study emphasizes AI's transformative impact across various sectors, in terms not just of speed but of fundamentally improving and redefining business practices and outcomes. The findings of this study were particularly intriguing as we explored whether the bold forecasts made by Reid Hoffman—that AI copilots would enhance every aspect of business operations by tenfold—and by Bill Gates would hold up under a rigorous, controlled experiment.

So, it's a big shift, and it's not a simple one. The research uncovers a complex terrain, where AI's capabilities are rapidly expanding yet remain unevenly distributed across different domains of knowledge work. This "jagged technological frontier" (as the paper's authors calls it) showcases AI's potential to significantly enhance or even replace human labor within its range of competence, while also highlighting the limitations and challenges that arise when its application extends beyond its current capabilities. In other words, the study found that

FIGURE 2-1

Navigating the jagged technological frontier: Field experimental evidence of the effects of AI on knowledge-worker productivity and quality

Incorporating AI into your decision-making is the new digital transformation—40% higher quality results, 25% more quickly.

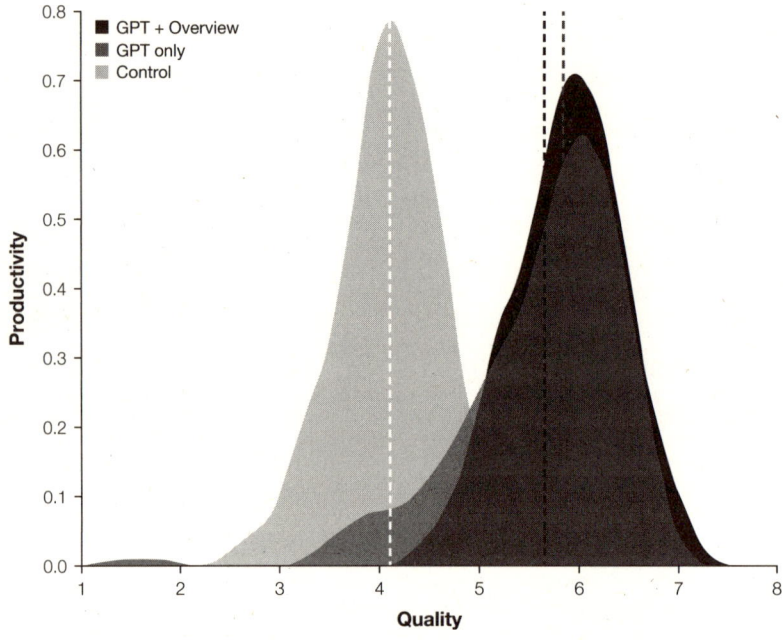

Source: F. Dell'Acqua et al., "Navigating the Jagged Technological Frontier: Field Experimental Evidence of the Effects of AI on Knowledge Worker Productivity and Quality," Harvard Business School Working Paper, no. 24-013, 2023.

despite the clear overall boosts to productivity (qualitative and quantitative), not every decision or activity or discipline was boosted through AI. This highlights the need for business leaders to be AI literate on some level and gain an understanding of where AI will likely be a great copilot and where it may be a poor investment.

The swift evolution of AI technologies, especially with advanced models like GPT-4, introduces a set of challenges in fully grasping the extent of their capabilities and the boundaries within which they operate most effectively. This rapid progression is not without its risks, and it underscores a critical need for professionals to adapt and to utilize AI with a nuanced understanding of its strengths and weaknesses.

One of the study's pivotal revelations is the impact of AI on high-skilled professional work, marking a departure from earlier forms of AI, which primarily automated lower-skilled jobs. LLMs are now reshaping tasks that require creativity, analytical thinking, and advanced writing skills, heralding a new era in which AI's influence permeates the upper echelons of professional expertise.

At the end of the Harvard/BCG paper, there was a discussion of the different styles of collaborating with AI to make better decisions: centaur versus cyborg behaviors as effective strategies for AI collaboration. The centaur approach advocates for a strategic division of labor, with humans and AI contributing distinctly yet collaboratively to achieve a common goal. Conversely, the cyborg behavior seeks a more integrated partnership, where AI's capabilities directly augment human efforts in real time, enhancing the immediacy and impact of task execution.

Interestingly, the study found that AI's assistance is particularly beneficial to less experienced workers, suggesting that AI can serve as a leveling tool that bridges skill gaps within the workforce. Looking forward, the study projects a significant transition in the workplace over the next three to five years, driven by the integration of AI. It calls on business leaders to reconceptualize AI not as a replacement for human talent but as a potent tool that can amplify human capabilities, particularly in areas that align with AI's inherent strengths. This shift necessitates a reevaluation of workforce strategies, urging a commitment to continuous learning and adaptation in the face of AI's rapidly evolving landscape.

. . .

The combination of the conversation with Gates and the Ethan Mollick study highlighted for us the uneven distribution of AI skills and knowledge and underscored a looming challenge—and opportunity—for businesses. It was becoming clear that those who invest in AI capabilities and upskill their workforce can leapfrog their competition, harnessing AI's power to drive innovation and efficiency. Those who don't invest may find themselves and their companies quickly falling behind and lagging.

As Gates aptly put it, "The risk for businesses that delay embracing AI is not merely falling behind; it's becoming obsolete." The Harvard/BCG study supports this, showing that early adopters of AI are not only streamlining operations but also much more likely to have an edge with regard to redefining customer engagement and marketing strategies.

At this point in our own AI journey, we felt compelled to revisit our mission at Forum3—and not only lean into AI for our product development, but really lean into the broader mission of empowering business leaders to harness the potential productivity gains of AI. As we talked through it with one another, we were reshaping even our own path. "We should see ourselves as the bridge between the current state of business and an AI first future," Adam explained to Andy. "How do we empower business leaders to be more AI proficient? How do we help them to embrace and get the most out of AI to unleash a competitive advantage through upleveling all aspects of their key tasks—starting with new ways to grow?"

Our vision is rooted in the belief that AI integration should be strategic and holistic. "It's not just about adopting a new tool; it's about rethinking how we approach business problems and opportunities," Andy responded to Adam.

We now had this new, wider mission in mind: empowering business leaders and marketers to be more AI proficient and AI first. Our next task was to do more on-the-ground research with business leaders themselves. So over the next month, we spoke to about a hundred leaders of all stripes: entrepreneurs, marketers, CEOs, salespeople. We posted on LinkedIn that we had some early learnings from our book research but wanted to talk to leaders about what they knew about generative AI, how they were using it, and how they viewed it. We also started reading research done by others on this same topic.

Two new studies from December 2023 stood out. The first, by Deloitte's AI Institute, came from interviews of 2,800 C-suite-level executives and found that only one in five executives believe their organization is highly prepared to address AI skill needs.[3] According to this study, a majority of executives said that their organizations were more focused on what AI could do to help reduce costs, but were failing to think of how AI could help create new types of growth.

The second study was from BCG and surveyed 1,400 C-suite executives.[4] In that study, 90 percent of the leaders said they were "waiting" for gen AI to move beyond its current state, and only experimenting with it in small ways. BCG called this 90 percent segment "observers." The BCG study revealed that observers were largely "ambivalent or dissatisfied" with their progress on gen AI.

Our own research and discussion with business leaders revealed much the same, but we were able to dive deeper. We found that 80 percent of the leaders we spoke with either didn't use ChatGPT regularly and/or used only the free version of ChatGPT-3.5. And of those using the technology, they were using it only occasionally, to write an email or job description. This group of self-described "low proficiency" gen AI users followed a similar pattern: they had a peripheral sense that gen AI must be able to do so much more for their businesses, but they didn't know how to harness its full potential. They were using it for writing productivity from time to time; and they *all* wanted to learn more about how to better incorporate gen AI into their workflow, but they didn't know where to start. It's the classic situation where you are aware that "you don't know what you don't know"—which is better than being totally ignorant, but can nonetheless leave you feeling paralyzed or helpless as to what to do next. And no one had the time or desire to spend a thousand hours learning this topic from podcasts, YouTube videos, X/Twitter, books, and the like.

We spent hours discussing and debating what would be the best way to help bridge that gap for business leaders. In many ways, this was familiar territory for us. It was a digital transformation. Andy literally founded organizations and companies that helped startups and titans like Microsoft go through a process like this; and Adam had been part of leading such transformations from the inside of household name brands, like Starbucks, and from his board seats at others. But this was somehow different. The technology here is so powerful, so general purpose, that it differed from those in our past experiences with how best to help organizations and leaders embrace and adopt a new type of technology. Unlike the technology in prior convergence eras, such as the web, social media, mobile apps, and cloud computing, this technology was more akin to having access to a team of experts at your fingertips. What do you do with that? Is it a tool, a new member of the leadership team, a process to adopt, or all of the above?

And what's more, the form the technology currently takes is haunt-ingly simple. It's just a blank input chat box, with a blinking cursor, staring at you, asking "How can I help you today?" Simple in its form, but with so many options, people can look at the blank chat box and wonder what to use it for. The temptation is to use it like a similarly simple user-interface design, a search box from Google or Bing, for example. But that's like hiring a research assistant, ghostwriter, or consultant, and asking them to tell you what the weather is like out-side. Sure, they can do it, but it doesn't begin to leverage their true potential. It was ironic. The most powerful software ever developed by humans, and it didn't even come with a user manual.

On the one hand, these foundational LLM interfaces didn't seem to need a manual—you just typed a question or request, and the LLM understood your natural-language prompt, and responded. Simple. On the other hand, there were prompting techniques that could help push the LLM to give you a much more powerful and helpful re-sponse. And what's more, you couldn't get value from an LLM at all unless you were even aware of what types of advice and analytical processes an LLM was capable of in the first place. Did the user even know that you can upload a document and ask the LLM to proofread and edit that document? Many did. But did you know that you can upload a spreadsheet, PowerPoint, or even just a PDF of a graph of a bunch of numbers, and it can parse, analyze, graph, interpret, and suggest next actions from that upload? Did you know that it can com-bine reading, browsing, and analysis in a single prompt request? Heck, did you know that it can strategize or find actionable insights from data summaries? Sometimes, none of those details matter. Other times, it's the difference between really leveraging the technology and missing the boat entirely.

So that brings us to where we are on our journey thus far. We now want to figure out what would be the most valuable, differentiated, and scalable way to help business leaders become AI proficient so they can optimize the way to leverage this new technology for their teams and their businesses. Clearly, this book, the book community, and any ancillary content would be part of it. But so would our company's software products. Could we develop a methodology and software system that could somehow plug into these powerful AI systems, or overlay them in a way such that these 80 percent to 90 percent of business-leader AI observers could cross the chasm into being AI leaders? What would that look like? That's where we will go next.

Chapter 3

THE MIDDLE ERA

Shortly after our meeting with Bill Gates, as the new year was upon us, we had the opportunity to speak with Jaime Teevan, Microsoft's chief scientist and technical fellow. It was part of a process of us broadening our discussions; we wanted not only to learn from generative AI CEOs and founders but also to mix in a variety of executives, thought leaders, and marketing leaders to triangulate our own journey with those of others. While it is incredibly helpful to hear directly from industry pioneers and leaders, it's just as important to understand how this technology is being rolled out at the application layer and/or understood and incorporated by leaders on the ground.

A technology that can't easily be understood or used won't have as much impact. Furthermore, a capability-enhancing technology that is unevenly being adopted can create competitive advantages and disadvantages between brands competing in the marketplace. Anyone building a brand would clearly want to wrap their head around this dynamic, so it has become our next focus area.

We didn't have a specific interview agenda in mind with Teevan; we didn't even know Microsoft had a chief scientist, or what that position entailed. All we knew is that Jaime Teevan worked at the intersection of generative AI and Microsoft's products. After speaking with Bill Gates, a man who talks in big pictures and grand thoughts, we wanted to talk to someone on the ground, as it were, and why not at the company Gates created? We knew Microsoft was all in on generative AI—it's hard to miss if you follow this sector—and we knew it had a close partnership with OpenAI, which meant the company was at the epicenter of all things AI. We were hoping Teevan could fill us in on what that meant.

In the summer of 2022, Teevan was making her short, two-mile drive home from Microsoft's Redmond campus when she suddenly and unexpectedly did something she had never done before. She pulled over and screamed. "Ahhhhh!" It was a spontaneous scream of amazement and excitement. For Jaime, this was out of character. She was a straight-shooting, smart, even-keeled researcher and executive at a major technology company. She didn't seem the type to exclaim randomly in her day-to-day.

What had Teevan yelling out loud to herself that day was the fact that she had just come from a demo at which she'd had an opportunity to try ChatGPT-4 for the first time, well ahead of its public release. And she knew right away that the technology and the product were different from previous incarnations of "AI," ones that had been promised (or at least teased) for so long. For a decade, every major tech company had visions of how it could bring AI to life, and it would seem, well, intelligent. The aspirations had always been ahead of the reality. It wasn't that previous versions of AI weren't amazing in many ways, but they fell short of something that you would say was humanlike or that possessed some general sense of computerized "intelligence." But this time, it was real. OpenAI had crossed that chasm between promise and reality when it came to the term *AI*.

At the time of seeing ChatGPT-4 herself for the first time, she had already been in her new role at Microsoft for about four years, working on research projects and experiments involving the intersection of Microsoft products and the future of work behavior. When the pandemic hit, in 2020, things started to get particularly interesting for Teevan, given that the entire world had entered into a huge, forced experiment that involved every knowledge worker working remotely simultaneously. The need to scale video conferencing, cloud-based infrastructure, and collaboration tools went from following a plodding, deliberate, tech-development track to being an essential and immediate demand. Teevan and her colleagues used the crisis to turn part of their attention to how AI could play a role to improve Microsoft's tools that were being used for remote work—especially for products like Office and its Teams collaboration platform.

As part of that effort, Teevan was given access to earlier versions of ChatGPT to help assess how Microsoft might incorporate AI into its core products. She was already quite impressed with how these large language models (LLMs) worked when compared with previous versions of "AI." When her colleague Kevin Scott asked her to meet with Sam Altman to play with ChatGPT-4, months before version 3.5 would be released for public use, he told her to be prepared to be blown away, just as Bill Gates had been a week earlier when he saw GPT-4 for the first time. Gates saw GPT-4 ace an AP biology exam, with added commentary from the LLM that proved it wasn't just memorizing answers but was truly "understanding" its answers.

But Teevan was a bit skeptical. Demos can be tailored to blow you away. Maybe what Gates saw was showing off a specialized, vertical-knowledge capability. She wasn't sure what to expect, but she went with an open mind.

She recalls how quickly any skepticism vanished at the demo. "For the first time it really had the ability to have a conversation with you," she recalled, "similar to all the years that we would talk about being able to incorporate an AI with an understanding of what you were saying, and could iterate, ask you questions, push back. It could handle conflicting constraints, ambiguity. You could point out where it was wrong or handled a question differently than you intended, and it would just adjust on the fly. It was really, really cool."[1]

As she drove home, she started to process what she had just seen. She started to think about the AI-to-core-product projects she was working on, and all of the projects she would work on next, and it hit her: Her job would never be the same again. ChatGPT and generative AI had clearly reached a capability level and usefulness that would change *everything*. Her mind raced with the implications. After all those years of anticipating and vectoring on what a truly intelligent and understanding AI could do, it was here.

"Ahhhhh!"

For so many people, they can tell you exactly where they were when they had that aha moment when it comes to generative AI. For almost everyone, it started with trying ChatGPT for the first time at the end of 2022 or early 2023. For us, it started building up from December 2022 with ChatGPT-3.5, and was solidified when we tried ChatGPT-4 ourselves a few months later; kicking off our AI journey, which for us is both literal and metaphorical, given that we actually decided to change our company's focus when we internalized what this technology would mean for the future of brand building, marketing, and customer engagement.

And, as documented in this book so far, you can see where that journey has taken us.

But then recently we had another aha moment—but it was more slow motion than the original aha moment of seeing GPT-4 for the first time. This time felt like being pushed deeper down a rabbit hole of realization, to another level. You know that feeling when you are already impressed with something and then realize it's just the beginning, not the peak, and your whole perspective changes? It's worth pausing and going through it here.

To start, one of our favorite podcasters and thought leaders in the AI space (and also founder and CEO of the Marketing AI Institute), Paul Roetzer, was kind enough to mention this book project on his podcast, *The Artificial Intelligence Show*. We had sent him the introduction and the first two chapters and were surprised and delighted that he brought up our book and our journey to his listeners. Paul did a double take when he read the quote from Sam Altman that started the book, the quote that changed the course of our own lives. You'll remember that Altman said that when artificial general intelligence (AGI) is here, 95 percent of today's marketing and creative tasks will be able to be accomplished via AI, almost instantly at practically no cost. He pegged the time frame as five years from now, possibly longer.

Paul was surprised that Altman had actually been willing to be so candid with us, not that the substance of the quote didn't jibe with his own understanding of what AGI would mean once it was really here. It caused Paul to step back and reflect on how he doesn't pause enough himself to ponder what's on the immediate horizon. In fact, on the following episode of his podcast, Paul led off talking about "the quote" again and walked through his own timetable of how he sees generative AI getting to AGI over the next five to ten years.

The quick summary of Paul's timetable looks like this:

- 2024: GPT-5, Gemini2-class models come into existence. Continued advancements in multimodal, reasoning, planning, decisioning, memory, personalization.

- 2025–2026: Multimodal AI explosion. Models become 10X to 100X more powerful and generally competent. AI devices such as glasses become more mainstream.

- 2025–2027: AI agents explosion—lots of actions can be taken more reliably without oversight. Disruption to knowledge work becomes more tangible and measurable.

- 2026–2030: Robotics explosion. Widespread commercial applications for AI robots. Tangible impacts on blue-collar work become more clear.

- 2028–2030: AGI emergence. Businesses reset across industries. One-to-ten-person, $1 billion-plus companies become common.

But before we could fully digest Paul's own thoughtful and substantive reflection and timeline, we happened to be listening to a relatively new podcast, *BG2Pod*, by Brad Gerstner and Bill Gurley, two successful investors that we admired. In that week's episode they were talking about the most current iterations and use cases of different neural-network models, starting with the use of these models for full self-driving Teslas. It was a fascinating listen around how Tesla changed its approach to AI for self-driving by moving to a more general neural-network and LLM-like approach, one where the model could just learn and understand from constantly uploaded driver videos how the car should drive itself.

Then Gerstner and Gurley continued their conversation about generative AI in a discussion about the much-rumored forthcoming launch of GPT-5. Gerstner said that his sources were reporting that ChatGPT-5 was already fully trained and was now just being "red teamed" (that is, fine-tuned and safety checked) before being released. And GPT-5 will be twice as powerful as GPT-4. And it's coming out in the next few months, if not sooner.

Wait. Twice as good?

We started discussing what it meant for something to be two times as good as the best thing out there. It was hard to get our heads around. Andy brought up the example of how people say that the new rookie NBA star Victor Wembanyama, aka "Wemby," is said to be 30 percent better than Michael Jordan, Lebron James, and Kobe Bryant at a similar stage of their rookie seasons. He can dribble, shoot, pass, and defend at their level, but he's also 7 feet 4 and is not supposed to be that good, and fast, and tall. But imagine if he were 100 percent better, not just 30 percent better. What would that even look like? As humans we can't get our brains around what it means to be two times better than something that's already very good. Think of your favorite dish at your favorite restaurant, and now try to imagine food twice as good and you will get what we were grappling with.

Over the course of just a few days, we could feel that our bearings were being shifted again. Like Paul Roetzer had, we became fixated on the vision of where this was all going someday (AGI), comparing that to the reality of the AI capabilities of today. We were focused on the proficiency gap for most leaders between today's AI capabilities and the leaders' current understanding, but we had almost lost sight of what was about to happen—lost sight of what likely will happen later *this year.*

And, just as we were wrapping our heads around that, we spoke with Mustafa Suleyman. And it was like an exclamation point on this disorienting feeling that we weren't focused enough on the next eighteen-month horizon.

Suleyman, like Sam Altman, Reid Hoffman, Bill Gates, and Jaime Teevan, is a renowned figure in AI research and implementation. He was part of the Google DeepMind founding team—the true early pioneers of the deep-learning and neural-network AI arena. Suleyman went on to cofound Inflection AI (with its product Pi) along with Reid Hoffman, and he was, at the time of our conversation, the CEO of Inflection AI and the author of the recent book *The Coming Wave* on the topic of AI.

Suleyman gave us a sense of a new era of AI that was coming quickly. "I think we are going to enter a new era soon that we could call 'ACI'—artificial competent intelligence," he said. "An era where the models are so good that they can competently handle almost any task. It isn't AGI, but it's a big step change from where we are now. And that's because the major research labs and foundational generative AI systems are applying (or about to apply) one hundred times the compute at the next version of their models. You can imagine what that means."[2]

We actually couldn't.

Suleyman continued, "For example, over the next year you will start seeing AI-based social media influencers that become famous, many as large as today's biggest influencers, but they will be completely AI—run by studios, companies, and entrepreneurs, of course, but totally AI in substance."

Well, that kind of felt like a non sequitur, slightly random, but that was the point. It made complete sense when you stopped and thought about what he was saying. If AI takes another major step forward in terms of its competence and capabilities, the implications are not just incremental. They will lead to some completely new realities. This example of influencers that are completely AI-created was something starting to happen already, particularly in Asia, but it was clear that Suleyman was waking us up to an example that was as jarring in the conversation as it might be in reality, when these things come to life.

Suleyman was intense. And to the point. He had something at work that he needed to attend to, so he had to reschedule the full interview, but we didn't get the impression that was the only reason for his intensity. He was in the middle of seeing decades of his life's work become an astonishing reality, and he understood it at a level few could relate to. No wonder he was like, *Yeah guys, you are right to feel a little unbalanced right now.*

After our truncated interview with Suleyman, we talked for hours just between the two of us about what this latest aha moment was all about. We had been so immersed in processing our first ChatGPT moment and the Altman AGI conversation that we didn't really stop and realize that the technology was likely to take another big leap forward this same year. Perhaps in just the next few months.

If we were feeling this way, and we are immersed in the subject every day trying to parse and understand what it all means, how would most other people be feeling? Or are most people even aware of what's happening? These technological advances are coming at us so quickly, it feels like we are on an exponential growth curve, and not a gradual, more-linear growth curve. And that could be leading to both our own disorientation and the growing proficiency gap in the marketplace.

But a proficiency gap—and a growing one at that—is something that can be tackled. We kept saying to each other that what it means is that leaders should be going from a code yellow to a code red when it comes to getting on top of this gap. Getting on top of it starts with understanding what is happening, and then developing a game plan for narrowing, or even closing, the proficiency gap for you and your team. And the first step to understanding what is happening is to step back and realize that it's natural for an emerging technology like this to feel like it's moving faster than anything you have seen before. Because it is.

It's human nature to feel that things will change in a linear and gradual fashion. After all, that's how most things develop. People age in a linear fashion. So do plants and animals. Most cities develop that way. As for technology, it's always been a little faster than that. But now we may be getting closer to the steep part of the curve on the exponential scale, and it's hard to figure out how to pace yourself. It reminded us of a conversation Bill Gates had on this topic with Sam Altman on the January 11, 2024, episode of Bill's YouTube/podcast show, *Unconfuse Me with Bill Gates.*[3] Gates remarked, "Unlike previous tech improvements, this one can potentially improve much faster than the past ones. And this one doesn't have an upper bound. It achieves human levels on a lot of levels of human work. You and I have some concern that it will force us to adapt faster than we have had to ever before."

"That's the scary part; not that people will have to adjust and adapt to technology revolutions," Altman replied. "We have always been able to adjust in the past. But these are happening faster than before, and what's scary now is the speed with which people will have to adapt to this one."

We were feeling that, and we quickly went into "What do we do about this?" mode. At work, our software platform, Spok, was already being developed to take advantage of ChatGPT-4 in a way that would let marketers and brand builders utilize this new technology in novel ways that went well beyond just chatting and collaborating. For example, our Spok platform combines ChatGPT-4's API application programming interface (API) with several sources of specialized data on search-keyword and web-traffic volumes, in such a way that marketers can come up with effective content marketing strategies and plans in a fraction of the time and with a fraction of the effort it normally takes. And while we were happy to be building software products along these lines, we also had an advisory-services line of business that focused on helping brands and marketers embrace and navigate these technologies. But in light of our newfound understanding of how fast this middle era of AI capabilities is approaching, we realized that we should ramp up our focus in the services area to accommodate what was likely to be an even bigger gap between the market's level of AI proficiency and the speed and capabilities of the technology itself.

So we set out to do two things: First, at our own company we wanted to start speaking with marketers and brand builders who were serious about an AI first digital-transformation agenda and who were taking action to help close the AI proficiency and usage gap for their own organizations. We felt that these conversations would be helpful for the book project, and for our own learning.

Second, we decided to launch an "AI first bootcamp" service at scale that would help brand builders and marketers jump-start their and their departments' own AI proficiency. We were getting the feeling there was about to be an explosive need for that, whether it was from us or the undoubtedly hundreds of firms that would offer something along these lines in the coming year.

. . .

Our first AI first digital-transformation conversation was with Eric Vaughan. Vaughan is a longtime technology entrepreneur. He is the CEO of IgniteTech and GFI Software, a set of companies that sell IT services and tools to businesses. Vaughan has a lot of energy and much to say about AI first digital transformation for his companies.

Vaughan sees generative AI in a line of major technology game changers: the internet in the 1960s and 1970s (TCP/IP), the personal computer in the 1970s and 1980s, the web in the 1990s, the iPhone in 2007, and now generative AI, starting with the ChatGPT moment in December 2022.

"I've seen these moments before," Vaughan said to us, "and I knew that if I saw another one come along, I wasn't going to waste a moment incorporating these into my companies' day-to-day work. That's because you either adapt and incorporate generative AI now or you will find yourself behind the curve and possibly out of business. It's that simple."[4]

And Vaughan did adapt, not wasting a moment. In early 2023, just after the launch of ChatGPT, at an all-hands meeting of his companies (which he effectively ran as a single company) to discuss the latest quarterly goals, Vaughan told his people, "This isn't going to be your typical quarterly all-hands. We are going to talk about how the world is changing and we have to change with it."[5] He explained that he was immediately instituting a new policy and program for *all* employees, to lead a culture shift toward becoming AI first. They would be "given a gift" of investment and support to learn AI and put it to productive use for the companies, but if there were a parting of the ways, that gift would keep on giving as both a skill and an awareness that those employees could take with them in their career.

He knew that many people would be skeptical and resistant. So he wanted to implement a program that didn't tolerate complete resistance. He said he would emphasize and reward his team for having the right attitude toward this new program and thus was looking for engagement as a first step. Vaughan gave his team several easy ways to engage with the new program he was rolling out, even if they didn't know how to be—or didn't want to be—AI proficient at a high level. Everyone just had to put in a good-faith effort. As Vaughan put it to us, "I've seen in the past how there can be so many skeptics, arms crossed, saying that they don't need to jump into the latest thing and how it's not for them. I wasn't going to let the skeptics create fear, uncertainty, and doubt for the rest of the organization by not participating in simple ways."

So, he put in a scoring system around how everyone engaged in the program. For example, he wanted everyone to submit tips on how to incorporate generative AI into the business. You scored points for any and all submissions. Easy enough. Good tips or bad tips, there was no wrong answer. Only if you didn't try would you get no points. He also encouraged participation in hackathon-type cross-functional projects involving generative AI. Top performers were given cash prizes (the top five received a $2,500 cash bonus), but the bottom performers who didn't try at all were considered in "the basement." And those in the basement were going to be asked to leave the company.

At the next quarter's all-hands meeting, Vaughan reported out that the tips and hackathon projects touched forty-three actual or potential products for the company, with twenty-six of them producing real code development already. Moreover, of all the tips submitted, 1,186 tips had been submitted with a projected $1.8 million business value associated with them. He also informed his team that those couple of employees in the basement had indeed been fired.

After initiating an ambitious AI first learning and engagement program, Vaughan took his commitment a step further in Q1 2024 with the introduction of "AI Mondays." This initiative mandated that every Monday be dedicated exclusively to AI education, projects, and product development across his global teams, no customer calls or work on other projects, with a zero-tolerance policy. Vaughan recognized the potential operational challenge in reallocating 20 percent of the business hours to AI, but as he told us, "We expected our teams to be solving that problem with their AI initiatives—after all, that's the entire aim, to 5X/10X actual business value. Gen AI is the most important change to the workplace perhaps of all time, and we are willing to invest in the efforts to ensure everyone treats it as a priority."

. . .

Vaughan's approach was action oriented, gamified, and one way to hit the ground running for a digital transformation of this sort. But we realized his method involved an extreme level of disruption to the business and was not likely to be the primary model companies, ones like yours, would take. We also wanted to find leaders who shared Vaughan's passion for AI first digital transformation but who were taking a less jarring approach.

Alicia Parker, CMO and managing director of one of the largest real estate companies and brands in the world, Tishman Speyer, provided a good case study of a more measured approach. Parker's team of marketers has the big job of telling stories, driving customer engagement, and running marketing and partnerships for hundreds of major properties all over the world, including iconic locations such as Rockefeller Center in New York City. Like Vaughan, Parker believes that organizations will quickly be divided into either AI first digital-transformation companies or laggards. As Parker told us, "We want to figure out the best way to get our team incorporating generative AI tools and processes into their daily work in the smartest way possible, because we believe it will give us an immediate competitive advantage in the marketplace as marketers."[6]

We pressed her on what she thought the tangible benefits of that kind of competitive advantage would look like. "I think the biggest challenge marketing has right now," she replied,

> is the changing landscape of technology and behavior alongside the multitude of marketing channels and touchpoints to attribute return on investment of marketing efforts. And I think that's an ongoing conversation that people are having. And so the more that we can connect and leverage generative AI for strategic business insights and the more that we can look into how we are going to actually use AI in our workflow, the more we will be able to deliver not just brand value as market-ers, but also real business value. If leveraged in a way that it can connect more deeply with our customers by kind of ramping productivity, cutting out the things that you do time and time again when you get projects up and running, you're able to then

make those projects better and better. And secondarily, I think there are aspects of it that over time will be cost reducing, but that will also enable you to then make strategic investments in things that you otherwise may not have, then grow the top line and help you engage differently with the consumer. So, my hope is it's doing both.

Parker is putting her whole team through a boot-camp process, where they quickly ramp up their AI proficiency through education, comparing notes and collaborating around AI use. It's a new type of training, given it's a new type of technology. It's about learning by doing, but in a general-purpose way—almost like a cohort approach, but the various constituents are all within the same organization, learning the same way, and collaborating and taking notes together. It has some of the same elements of Eric's approach, but it's more focused on individual and group proficiency, and learning by doing as you go.

. . .

Those are two examples of leaders adopting an AI first digital-transformation approach in their organizations. Different levels of intensity, but the same overall intent and inspiration. We wondered what others were doing, so we asked Paul Roetzer, the cohost of *The Artificial Intelligence Show* podcast, and the one who mentioned this book on his show. He has coauthored a bestselling book, *Marketing Artificial Intelligence*, with Mike Kaput (who cohosts his terrific weekly podcast).

Paul could quickly give examples of where companies were *not* doing it well. In those examples, the company or the leaders were treating generative AI like any other technology implementation. They would bring in their CTO or CIO and it would be treated like a data project or SAAS software implementation. Which, on some levels, is relevant from a confidentiality, liability, and security standpoint. But it seems to miss the mark and the opportunity on how to think of this technology strategically, not as just an implementation but a digital transformation—a mindset shift.

"The best examples we've seen are the people who take our guidance, which is education and training is first and foremost," Paul said.

> You have to level up with the team and their understanding of generative AI, because to start with, many people are afraid for their jobs. They have no idea what this tech really does. So you have education and training first, and then they really need to get an AI council in place that thinks this through for your company, your industry. Like, what are the implications? You need generative AI policies, responsible AI principles. You need to do an AI impact assessment. No one's doing this yet, but leaders need to ask, 'What is the impact of this on our team twelve months from now?' Do we need as many writers, as many SEO people, as many accountants? Is AI going to reduce the number of humans that are needed to do the work?
>
> And then the next step is to build an AI road map. What are the pilot projects we should be running? What are the problems we should be trying to solve more intelligently? We are seeing a lot of progress on the pilot-project phase, like they're going and getting a tool and trying to figure out if it works, but they're not really doing it properly. For example, it would be good to have someone own the pilot project, benchmarking performance

before and after, setting a ninety-day limit on it; not paying for a twelve-month agreement with some new AI tool until you've proved it's going to work after ninety days.[7]

Paul was validating not only our thoughts on the growing proficiency gap between brand builders and marketers when compared with the speed of AI technology development, but also our belief that the best practice for leaders was to think of this as a transformation moment for their organization and to develop a thought-through approach to implementing and leveraging AI in their workflow.

. . .

In our journey thus far, this latest series of conversations and realizations felt the most whirlwind-like, but also the most cohesive. On the one hand, it feels like we are about to enter a new era with the launch of GPT-5—a sort of middle era between the emergence of GPT-4 a year ago (along with Claude, Gemini, Mistral, and others over the past year) and what full-blown AGI might be like five-plus years from now.

This new middle era between GPT-4 and AGI will likely usher in a true paradigm shift around generative AI being so much more than just a customer-service bot, research assistant, or writing assistant. Enterprises are likely to realize that having a real plan for incorporating generative AI into almost everything they do isn't really a choice if they want to remain competitive, and most leaders will start to ramp up their urgency for cultivating an AI first digital-transformation muscle.

And while there is a spectrum of ways to do that, from Alicia Parker's approach to Eric Vaughan's approach, there is clearly a best-practices playbook for how to start down this road. To summarize that approach as Paul explained it to us:

1. Get yourself and your company AI educated and proficient.

2. Understand what's happening in the space and have a point of view about your need to embrace it.

3. Assemble an AI council and/or designate an AI leader in your organization.

4. Get an AI use policy in place.

5. Start preparing and launching AI pilots with clear goals and assessment.

6. Start your AGI horizon planning.

It feels like the next step in our journey is going to revolve around us diving into this playbook with a variety of companies and leaders. It feels like we all might need to get a running start as this new middle AI era quickly approaches.

Part Two

WHAT SHOULD I DO ABOUT IT?

Chapter 4

AI FIRST MARKETING

I t's time to take a breath.

When we start to think about what we have learned and where we are heading, it's not exactly going to feel like that's easy. Maybe it's more apt to say it's a good time to *step back* and consider the implications of what we have been learning here.

On our AI journey so far, we have had the unique and fortunate opportunity to hear from some of the most important, most influential, and most prescient leaders in this rapidly emerging generative AI space. We have asked them to shed some light on what's possible, what's likely, and when it's going to happen—all related to gen AI's emergence. We have been going from leader to leader, from discussion to discussion, and just letting the journey unfold organically from one (breathless) chapter to the next.

We started this process with a specific goal: to learn what the emergence and rapid progression of generative AI would mean for brand builders and marketers in particular. We hoped that in the process of getting to that goal, what we learned and distilled would also be of general value to business leaders from all functions and business types. But as you can see from our chapters so far, we quickly got pulled down the rabbit hole of what generative AI would mean writ large for companies, leaders, and even society, in a more general sense. With the community's encouragement during the serialization of this book, we did this because we realized it's what they needed before we could get into the tactical implications of AI.

In this chapter we start getting tactical, taking what we have learned so far that directly bears on the topic of marketing and brand building. In other words, *what is the future of marketing in this emerging AI first world?* And in the spirit of stepping back, let's spend at least this one chapter just digesting, observing, and drawing predictions from the conversations thus far, and not center the chapter on a specific interview or two.

Branding and Marketing in the AI Era

To try to answer what the future of marketing might look like, let's review what the job of a marketer consists of today: it's a job in the conventional sense that it is made up of several jobs to be done that will almost certainly still exist as we move into an AI first world. But *how* those jobs get done is likely to change tremendously.

Let's dig into what we mean by that by listing the basic building blocks of marketing jobs to be done today. Table 4-1 offers a comprehensive list and intentionally includes a breakdown of each area, as we wanted to point out all the individual tasks that make up each section.

As you can see, each one of these areas includes bundles of tasks that make up the job to be done. This is true of many functions, not

TABLE 4-1

Marketing jobs to be done

Market research

- Consumer-behavior analysis
- Sentiment analysis
- Market segmentation and targeting
- Trend identification

Content creation

- Blog-post and article writing
- Video-content scripting and production
- Infographic and visual content creation
- Social, web, and email content creation

Email marketing

- Email campaign design and automation
- Segmentation and personalization
- A/B testing for emails
- Performance analysis and optimization

Sales enablement

- Sales-collateral creation
- Lead scoring and prioritization
- Integration with CRM systems
- Sales-performance analytics

Regulatory compliance and data privacy

- Data-protection regulations
- Privacy-policy enforcement
- Compliance tracking and reporting

Competitive analysis

- Competitor benchmarking
- SWOT analysis
- Pricing-strategy analysis
- Product-feature comparison

SEO and SEM

- On-page, off-page SEO optimization
- Keyword analysis and strategy
- Pay-per-click campaign management
- Link-building strategy

Advertising

- Ad creation and testing
- Target-audience identification for ads
- Media-buying and planning
- Ad performance analysis

Customer-relationship management

- Customer segmentation
- Customer-journey mapping
- Personalized marketing campaigns
- Loyalty-program management

Integration and automation

- API integrations with marketing tools
- Workflow automation across tools
- Real-time data syncing

Strategy development

- Marketing-mix modeling
- Campaign-strategy development
- Budget-allocation and ROI forecasting
- Brand positioning and messaging

Social media marketing

- Social media strategy, calendar planning
- Audience-engagement analysis
- Influencer-partnership management
- Reputation management

Public relations

- Press-release drafting and distribution
- Media outreach, relationship management
- Crisis-management planning
- Event promotion and management

Analytics and reporting

- Dashboard creation
- Data visualization
- Campaign-effectiveness analysis
- Market-insights and -forecast reporting

User experience and interface

- Website and app usability testing
- Conversion-rate optimization
- A/B testing for UI/UX

just marketing. But as with many other functions, when you see the list broken down like this, you can imagine how each individual task might be able to be accomplished by AI systems in the future, especially if the technology continues to progress at even close to its current pace.

So, in general, we can see why there is so much conversation around how AI could potentially take over certain marketing jobs in the future. There is rightly a lot of fear and concern over this point. However, as we will cover in this chapter, the reality is likely to be much more nuanced than just AI taking over jobs. It'll be more about changes in the nature of the job marketing is doing for your organization and the roles of the people in marketing when AI truly gets infused into the marketing and creative function over the next few years.

To start, let's just state that the ultimate purpose of a marketing or creative job (and its bundle of tasks) will likely stay consistent over time. That is, it will transcend the transition into an AI first world. Irrespective of how much AI changes the landscape of what's possible—or even changes the nature of the consumer landscape—marketers will still need to perform research and analysis, come up with a content strategy, create content, and implement campaigns across a variety of channels. Could you leave *all* of these tasks to computers in the future? Maybe. Would it be effective? Time will tell.

That said, over the next few years, a lot will change around this core transcendent fact. The channels the consumers are using will likely change. The products being marketed might also change some. And even the marketing job titles and scopes are likely to change, as we will talk about at the end of this chapter.

After reviewing everything we have learned thus far on our journey, it seems that most of the big changes for marketers in an AI first world will fall into three main areas:

- Creativity

- Productivity

- Personalization

Let's take each in turn.

Creativity

When we talk about the concept of creativity generally, we usually think of this as being a purely human domain, safest from the emerging AI world. While we are used to imagining and experiencing how computers, aided by machine learning, can help with calculations and repeatable tasks and functions, we often have trouble getting our head around the idea of machines being as creative as a human. Early efforts—by this we mean efforts of just a few years ago—by AI to be creative were often comical and reinforced our sense that computers just can't write scripts, or ad campaigns, or music.

To better understand why we think in this way, it's worth digging into the specifics of what creativity means in the context of marketing. For marketers, creative output usually consists of text/copy, images, and videos that are used in emails, on your website, on your social media posts, and in your digital and physical ads. And a level up from creative output, the concept of creative strategy—often based on data, research, competitive analysis, instinct, experience—is also a form of a creative output.

WHAT SHOULD I DO ABOUT IT?

There is obviously both an art and a science to producing great creative output and strategy. The copy, images, and video need to elicit the right emotional response in the intended audience. Someone needs to have an idea of what kind of message and feeling to create, and to whom it should be targeted, and the best channel to use. This is the science part of the equation—and is based on research, data, and analysis. Then comes the art: an artist or designer and/or writer needs to actually produce the right creative output to create the most powerful form of that emotional response.

But what makes this output right is a combination of subjective aspects of whether the creative is on brand, whether it effectively conveys the intended message, and whether it strikes the right chord with the consumer. It's this latter aspect of striking an emotional response that we usually intuitively assume must be the domain of humans. Striking emotional chords requires skills like intuition, humor, empathy, and similar traits, so it's understandable to assume AI would struggle in this area—especially given its difficulties with such tasks not long ago.

But what's so intriguing about the current AI models—both the large language models (LLMs) and diffusion models—is that they can do *both* the science and the art. They can analyze and predict what the desired creative should look like and act like, and why. And they can also physically create the digital pixels and sound waves of the creative itself. The former by using LLMs and a variety of ancillary tools, think ChatGPT-4o and Claude 3 and Gemini 1.5, and the latter by using diffusion models such as Dall-E 3, Sora, Midjourney, and the like. These new diffusion models can not only create incredibly evocative images, videos, and voice/music but can also be quite creative and novel and weird about it, if we ask them to. And they can create consistent characters, and even be edited. All through simple natural language text prompting.

And if you think these AI systems can't produce a truly unique or emotionally powerful new idea, concept, or strategy, think again. Remember, the deep neural networks upon which the foundational LLMs and AI systems of today are based are incredibly human-like in their ability to come up with innovative new solutions and concepts. And while they draw on a wealth of previously expressed ideas from their training (just like a human would unconsciously draw on all of the ideas and creative expressions they have been exposed to in their life), AI systems can also come up with new creative ideas too.

A famous example of this comes from outside the marketing realm. One of the earliest examples of generative AI breakthroughs came in 2016, when a deep-learning-based AI system called AlphaGo played the best Go player in the world (Lee Sedol) and did something no one expected. In the pivotal second game of their historic match—with the eyes of the world watching—AlphaGo made an unexpected, even shocking move, which today people call "move 37." It was a move no one had ever seen or considered before, and it won the game for the AI system. Many thought it was a mistake at first, but it has widely been touted since as a showcase for these AI systems having a capacity for creativity and intuition previously thought only possible in humans. There was no example of this kind of a nonobvious and genius move being made before. It showed a spark of creative and novel thinking by an AI system.

Flash forward to today's AI systems, which are even more powerful than what was possible in 2016, and we see consistent evidence of this phenomenon. Studies published recently in *Scientific Reports* and *Nature* compared the performance of foundational LLMs against hundreds of human participants in the area of creative thinking and solutions and found that the AI chatbots achieved higher scores than humans for originality and divergent-thinking tasks designed to measure creativity. (It should be noted that the very top percentile creative answers still came from the humans, but on average AI was deemed more creative in its ideation and output.)

And, keep in mind, for at least another three years or so these models will continue to improve in terms of intelligence, creativity, and capabilities. It's why OpenAI's Sam Altman feels that artificial general intelligence (AGI) is achievable in the next five years or so, depending on your definition. He's not alone in that opinion among top AI leaders. And it's a logical take when you follow the path of improvement and what's causing that improvement. So far, all of the major foundational LLM models have followed what are called scaling laws—meaning that the more compute and data is applied to the pretraining process for the model, the better the model performs. And these improvements may actually be exponential, not linear. We know that every one of these major foundational-model labs are already up to over $1 billion in compute being applied to training whatever the forthcoming model version will be—and that number is going into the multiple billions for some of them. Add to that the vast sums of data that Meta, Google, and others can still add to the training mix (not to mention the possibility that models can train on synthetic data produced by the AI systems themselves), plus improved fine-tuning, and it stands to reason that we will continue to see better and better models with every passing year, quarter, and month.

Given that the path generative AI systems are on continues to improve, and given that AI is already very capable of putting science and art together for creative output, you don't need much imagination to see that we're heading toward a world where the majority of creative output for marketing activities will be handled by AI-based creatives and designers. These AI-based creatives and designers will still be managed by humans (or AI editors), but it's not hyperbolic to say that creativity and creative output in the marketing domain will be squarely disrupted and will shift to be primarily AI-based over time.

But this disruption and transformation isn't just one way. Yes, AI can take on a huge swath of the creative output implemented by humans today. But AI can also *help* humans be more creative, not just do some of the creative work for them. In fact, it seems that AI is most powerful when it's a thought partner for the human driving the process; coproduction versus just doing the work for them. There are numerous research papers that show that AI helps the lowest-performing knowledge workers even more than the highest-performing knowledge workers. The studies have been more centered on somewhat objectively measurable knowledge-work outputs, like strategies and plans for marketing a new product. But it stands to reason that the same applies to creative output. AI is a proven thought partner, sound board, and idea generator. And we know it can be creative. It stands to reason that AI will not just disrupt creativity by doing the job, so to speak, but will also be a cyborg partner to the human creator.

Remember, in chapter 2 we talked about how a Harvard Business School/Boston Consulting Group study showed that the use of gen AI in knowledge work resulted in a 40 percent qualitative gain and a 25 percent quantitative gain, and some of the best results occurred when the human and AI worked together, back and forth, to get to a better result—what the paper referred to as the cyborg method of using AI. It stands to reason that this cyborg approach to partnering with AI applies to a creative-output process as much as it does to insights—or decisioning-based work. In our own experience, we have seen several examples of marketing leaders using a combination of an AI-driven brief-response prompt to produce a variety of creative strategies, followed by the use of AI image or video tools to quickly create a mood board or rapid prototyping of creative output against those proposed strategies. In this example process, the brand marketer can get a much wider canvas of ideas either to be inspired from or to create derivative original works from.

Productivity

So much of the work done by marketers today involves tedious, time-consuming, but vital tasks, consisting of research, planning, piecing together content plans, executing on those plans, and measuring and reporting results to the rest of the business. As mentioned above, marketing jobs are often a bundle of tasks, and for most marketing jobs (content marketing, social media management, growth marketing, brand marketing) those tasks fall into well-worn buckets: market research, competitive analysis, keyword research, content planning, and then overseeing content creation and deployment across owned, earned, and paid channels. This all takes a lot of time and effort, much of which must be done sequentially, and with a fair bit of trial and error.

What if AI could not just help with marketing insights, decisions, and creative output but could actually take on *doing* many of the tasks that make up the job?

This is where AI agents are likely to come into play. An AI agent refers to the idea of an LLM that not only can understand your prompt/input and can generate content in response but can actually take an *action* on your behalf as well. In simple terms, think of it as the difference between just helping you to learn about a destination and plan a vacation and *actually booking* the flights and hotel rooms and paying for them on your behalf. The booking of the flight is an agentic part, powered by an underlying LLM.

These AI agents will have all of the intelligence and creative capabilities just discussed *and* be given goals and authority by us to do what we ask them to do. Want an AI personal assistant that can read emails, reply to emails, and actually book meetings for you? AI agents will be able to accomplish that. Will they be able to post content on social media and place digital ads for my company based on segments and data that allow for personalized or targeted posts? Yes. Book a vacation or work trip for me, including flights, hotels, rental cars? You get the idea.

AI agents, powered with smart underlying language models, connected to the internet, and fully multimodal, are purported to be the next big wave of features we can expect to be released from all major AI systems. These agents will be able to do many, many tasks that comprise a wide range of jobs, including the long list of marketing jobs listed earlier in this chapter. As a result, AI systems will unlock the ability to achieve better results in the areas of customer acquisition, retention, and frequency, and do so while allowing for less staff, faster output, and greater volume.

And remember our discussion in chapter 2 about the multiple dimensions of how AI helps with productivity. It's not just about doing more with less, but also about optimizing the output quality because you have this new resource and process enhancement. That will likely be true of creative-output quality as much as any other type of knowledge-work output. Thinking of the high-level marketing task of analytics, for example, it's easy to imagine the positive knock-on effects of AI. One of the most tedious and difficult parts of data analysis is cleaning and verifying data. Many wrong decisions are made based on datasets with dirty noise or poor organization. Using AI to ensure you're working with accurate, high-quality data allows data analysts to focus more on analysis rather than data management.

This step change in productivity for marketers will likely cause a shift in the expectations of business leaders. Today, when a CEO, CMO, or business owner thinks about the resources and expectations of ROI from their marketing teams and agencies, they often are confronted with the reality that their teams don't have enough resources to cover all the bases when it comes to data analysis, insight gathering, and creative production. And the ROI isn't clear enough to just throw more dollars at it in the hope it will produce better results. But in the next few years, the expectation of business owners and CMOs will likely shift from scarcity to abundance given the productivity lift these systems are capable of providing.

Personalization

Targeting consumers in a truly personalized way has long been the holy grail for marketers. Most marketing campaigns are broken into just a few variations, if that, and then each campaign variation is "targeted" or "matched" to a segment of customers via a publishing platform. The closest most marketers have come to scalable personalization is targeted ad campaigns through programmatic, targeted, paid digital advertising on platforms like Facebook, Instagram, TikTok, YouTube, and the like. But that's more about making sure that maybe a few (if that) posts/ads are reaching the right audience and segment.

That's less about hypersliced, multisegment content reaching the right audience with a tailored message and creative output. That is what true personalization looks like.

But why is true personalization a holy grail, and not an everyday marketing tactic by most brands? The reason lies with the huge effort it takes to do the AI-based analysis to create the right segments, and then produce all of the creative that would be necessary to fill all of those content slots, and then to execute on getting that creative in front of the targeted customers—and on top of all of that, you need to measure performance and wrap that back into the next round. And yes, there would be round after round. Marketers generally don't have a big staff, and don't have access to agencies—how are they going to do all of that? Are they going to ask their technology departments to build a system for them to do that? Not likely. That tech department is usually swimming in tech debt on data systems, infosec, web, and mobile UX, let alone enterprise-system tech debt. So true personalization usually remains a latent opportunity for most marketers.

But that's likely about to change. Taking what we have learned about today's AI systems, it's not hard to imagine a marketer just speaking a chain-of-thought prompt exercise to the AI system to run:

Hey AI system. I would like you to spend the next few moments focusing on the top three highest-potential customer segments based on matching psychographics to our top-performing customers and based on your research with our synthetic AI-based persona, and then I would like you to spin up a team of creative agents to create content, messaging, and pricing that is most likely to convert at an optimal return on ad spend against those segments. And after asking another team of AI proofreaders and testers to go over the output and optimize, I would like you to post these ads on a cross section of social media, web, and AI-based search platforms most likely to see a strong likelihood of usage from these target segments. Please use the provided budget and ROI guidance uploaded here, and then report back to me on a twice-a-day basis on performance and adjustments over the next two weeks.

But that's just getting after today's definition and paradigm of personalization. That definition might change and expand very quickly. We are very likely heading to a world where consumers are already interacting with a variety of AI systems that are personalized in that they are one-to-one live conversational interactions between the consumer and an AI-system-powered application. As a marketer, your context and paradigm are likely to shift from trying to figure out how to target an ad to a segment, to trying to figure out how to make your ad come to life with the audience in a personalized, customized, and interactive way. That wasn't possible until now and is a totally new way of framing up the art of marketing going forward.

Let's give some examples of what that world might look like.

The very nature of what constitutes a digital ad is likely to morph into something unrecognizable. If a fully intelligent and interactive AI system can interact with you on-the-fly for customer-support needs, then you can imagine an ad unit doing the same. Imagine you are watching YouTube or Instagram Reels in the future and the stream gets interrupted with an ad, but instead of it just streaming something targeted to you, you are suddenly being asked by an AI spokesperson if you have heard of this or that new product. Game publishers already advertise in this way on touchscreen devices (phones and tablets), where the ad unit is actually an interactive sample of the game. With new AI systems, this could happen for video ads as well. For a sports fan, you could be watching a stream of an NFL game, when at the commercial break, instead of another humorous ad video for State Farm, an AI version of Jake from State Farm or Travis Kelce engages you in a conversation about something fun and relevant. They could even use AI agent capabilities to send you a quote, compare your current rates, or even just engage with you about something related to football that makes you more connected to State Farm, but isn't directly selling you on the company's product. This is almost possible with today's AI technology, let alone with the next few years' worth of progressions.

And on top of the concept of living ads, there is likely to be an AI-driven trend toward highly customized entertainment and productivity content. Customized content is highly personalized. Besides perhaps watching Netflix on their Apple Vision Pro in massive widescreen and surround-sound effect, many consumers will be watching custom movies and listening to custom songs as we move into an AI first era over the next five-plus years. When they go to the gym, they might have their AI personal trainer help them. For school and education, we are also likely to see an explosion of AI personal tutors.

We just mentioned the concept of custom movies and songs, so it's worth double clicking on this topic. What do we mean by that, and how close is it to reality? It's already a reality today for music. There are platforms like Suno and Udio that allow you to type in a description of the genre, tempo, vocal style, and lyrical theme, and they will instantly (in less than twenty seconds) create a completely new song (even with album-cover artwork, created by AI, of course). Putting aside for a moment whether the training for these platforms will be considered legal or ethical (same question applies for LLMs generally, as well as the AI image- and video-creation platforms), the fact that the technology exists today is worth pausing over and noting. You can literally create your own favorite music if you want to. It's only a matter of time before this is possible for videos too. And we know it's already possible for art and photography, with the likes of Midjourney, Dall-E, and Llama. Custom creative content, on the fly.

For custom movies, that's still farther out, but not total science fiction. OpenAI and Google have both previewed their text-to-video tools: Sora and Veo, respectively. Each already can produce nearly thirty-second clips of perfectly lifelike videos instantly from just a brief text description. Storyboarding, editing, voiceovers, and background-music features are already being built for these systems. It doesn't take a big leap to imagine that custom videos, documentaries, and shows will follow today's custom-music capabilities over the next phase as AI progresses.

So, the definition and concept of personalization will change due to all this progress. There will still be today's definition of personalization (even the holy-grail version of it), and it will likely become democratized (or at least unlocked) through AI systems doing the science, art, and agentic work for marketers. And then there will be this new, live personalization that happens when ads come to life and can be programmed to interact with the customer in a customized manner, much like AI trainers, tutors, companions, and spokespeople will be doing every day.

But before moving off personalization, it's important to note that the same forces that can produce highly customized ads, and even ads that come to life, could also drive a huge rise in the potential for AI-powered disinformation, scams, and deepfakes. All the advances in AI systems that we have alluded to and that will come to pass in the next five years will be in the hands not just of the consumer but also the scammer and thief. The ability for criminals, scammers, and unethical individuals to create persuasive phishing attacks, and deepfakes of colleagues, friends, and family, and to just generally promote misinformation for whatever selfish purpose, will be at an all-time high. Already *today* AI allows anyone to create perfectly real-seeming photos, videos, and voice recordings of moments that didn't occur. They are astonishingly convincing. And that's with today's technology.

The average consumer, therefore, will likely be on guard—highly attuned to wanting to filter and verify content and to approach it with a much more critical eye than one does today. It's possible that tech can help here—perhaps the equivalent of next-generation spam filters for almost all content consumed. But that's hard when it comes to social media that you pull (versus being pushed to you), or other sources of news.

So as marketers, we will need to be strategic and innovative in the ways that we make these custom or interactive ads punch through the noise and skepticism of a consumer who will constantly be in a defensive state. Consumers might feel exhausted, and this will require that ads be approachable, authentic, and feel real. Those ads and campaigns that clear that bar may carry a large premium when it comes to marketing effectiveness, in ways that today's marketing and advertising doesn't need to accomplish.

Managers of AI Systems

But what does this all mean to the job of the marketer if, within the next five years, the marketing bundles of tasks can likely be performed by AI, with just a little guidance, 95 percent of them, anyway?

We predict that marketing will become more about setting goals, monitoring budgets, giving context, providing some feedback (although there will be feedback AI agents for that too), iterating, and optimizing. It will also mean that the definition/scope of the marketer might change along with this—in this new world, marketers will be managers of AI systems. But that doesn't necessarily mean a ton fewer marketers and agencies (although that's a distinct possibility). It could also mean that marketers get to do so much more than they get to today with current resources and capabilities. Think about it—for most marketers, they can't possibly get to half of the items on the list of jobs to be done. Most can't afford a big staff. And nearly none can afford talented marketing and creative agencies. Now they will have a "staff" of AI marketers, and access to what feel like "AI agencies." There will be plenty for them to do to manage these systems. But it will require new expertise, skills, and capabilities as marketing *managers*. You can't just tell an AI system to do something that you don't understand what you are asking for any more than you can ask a human-based staff or agency to do that.

Suddenly skills that may have been less important for today's marketer become most in demand. The ability to be a strategic thinker and to direct, delegate, review, and optimize might become more salient and in demand for tomorrow's marketing skill set. Marketers who become familiar with AI-system capabilities would become more valuable and capable than ever before, as the world of effective marketing moves from humans doing almost all the tasks to AI systems doing the tasks with humans directing the work.

It's not a simple shift to get your head around, granted. As we said at the beginning of the chapter, taking a step back wasn't going to be easy. But take heart. This isn't going to be a total retraining or different job altogether. It's just going to emphasize the skills around strategy, management, delegation, reviewing, and understanding the power of these systems—all aimed at the same overall job-function goals, as we stated above. And it will feel like an environment of abundance, not scarcity. We aren't sugarcoating the level of disruption and on some level displacement, but we are choosing to view the glass as half full. As technology and digital-transformation leaders, we have seen time and time again how these types of shifts tend to lead to more opportunities and innovative successes for functional leaders who are willing to lean in and embrace the new technology with curiosity and vision. For marketers and creatives who do so, this may be a once-in-a-lifetime opportunity to relaunch or amplify their careers.

Chapter 5

AI FIRST MINDSETS

I t should be noted, if you're reading this as a book and weren't part of the community that helped shape it serially, that we hit another pivot point when we got to this chapter.

We saw two paths forward with the rest of the book. And we put both to the community. One path was for the book to continue to look at the technology itself, and go even further into marketing and brand-building tactics that flow from these projections. Basically, continue to be futurists, hearing from top minds and speculating on near- and long-term change that will come to businesses and brands.

The other path would take us in a different, more holistic direction—one that comes at the topic more from the perspective of the reader who says, "OK, you have my attention, I'm grokking the implications, but what does this mean for my brand or organization?" In that vein, we would try to elucidate specific examples of what to do about *all this*. We'd give you case studies from various brands and leaders who have come to the same conclusion as we have about where this is heading and have already decided to shift their mindset and approach to running their organizations and building their brands.

We chose the latter path, and the community supported this fully. And here's why.

If you go back to the beginning of this book, Sam Altman's notion that 95 percent of marketing could be handled by AGI within five years raises this same pressing question: "What do we do about that now?" The uncertainty of the next few years highlights the need for a new mindset and playbook to navigate this inflection point.

As we have been speaking with business leaders over the past few months, including those who have been reading along and reflecting on our AI journey, it has become clear that each of the interviews included in the book revealed significant aha moments, moments where industry leaders like Reid Hoffman, Bill Gates, and others were struck by the power of this new technology and its near-term ramifications. To these leaders—and to us!—it was clear that this moment in time felt like a call to action. This is true, by the way, to the point that we even advocated to our publisher that we title the book *The Holy Shit Moment: The AI Playbook for Businesses and Brands*. While it liked the spirit of the title, our publisher tucked that title into the introduction to the book and encouraged a different approach for the broader market.

That different approach to the title was to focus more on the answer to the question of, *What now? A call to action to do what?* This chapter marks the transition from our AI journey to yours. Now we start building the playbook for *how* you become AI first.

We've chosen that title, *AI First*, and the subtitle of the book, with input from our community of readers who have been following and participating in the conversation around what AI means to businesses, brands, and leadership. It's a title that reflects the first part of the answer to the call to action—a mindset shift and a playbook that fits your organization for how to incorporate generative AI into the fabric, culture, and everyday process of how you build your brand.

We want to instill a sense of urgency. AI is transforming the world *now*, and business leaders have been generally slow to respond to this significant change. In fact, everyone has been, including not just businesses but employees, and governments as well. Our belief—shared by most of the people we've interviewed—is that action is needed now to harness AI's transformative power.

Despite the uncertainties, and some of the fearful coverage of AI, we see more opportunity than threat—though we recognize the presence of both. AI offers unprecedented opportunities to enhance productivity, creativity, and decision-making. It can significantly augment human capabilities and drive innovation across industries. However, we cannot completely ignore the challenges, such as ethical considerations, job displacement, climate implications, and the need for new skills and adaptability.

Throughout our journey, we have been working closely with business leaders—CEOs, CMOs, and CROs—to figure out the best response to this pivotal moment. By understanding the current capabilities of AI and anticipating its future developments, businesses can strategically integrate AI to enhance decision-making, creativity, and operational efficiency. But two things are key:

- Start now.

- Put AI first.

Our narrative underscores the importance of both imperatives to stay competitive. As AI continues to evolve, the lessons from our journey should provide a road map for business leaders to navigate this transformative landscape, ensuring they harness AI's full potential to drive innovation and maintain a competitive edge.

Introducing an AI First Mindset Shift

AI first is both a mindset and a playbook. Let's start with the mindset. And perhaps it might be good to start with the individual mindset before trying to tackle the organizational mindset as we click into what we mean.

For example, when Andy's son Jude asked for career advice, we encouraged him to explore AI as a baseline for his next steps. No matter your chosen career, whether it's in tech or the arts or anything else, this will benefit you. Jude, who is at the front end of his career, took the approach that if he brought AI to the table for almost all his tough decisions, brainstorming, and planning, it would personally give him an edge. Two years later, Jude uses AI for college assignments and internship duties, significantly boosting his productivity. This rapid skill acquisition and deployment is happening globally with AI and large language models (LLMs).

AI-proficient individuals like Jude use AI as their assistant, almost like taking a professional "limitless pill." (See the movie *Limitless*, starring Bradley Cooper, where he takes a pill that allows him to harness his entire brain's capabilities and he is able to make an order of magnitude improvement in his cognitive abilities, and hence he achieves incredible success in almost everything he works on.)

According to Wharton School Professor Ethan Mollick's study, "Navigating the Jagged Technological Frontier," young professionals with an AI first mindset are supercharged to compete across all functional and industrial capacities.[1] This trend is driven from the bottom up, with young professionals leveraging AI to complete work faster, take personal time, and deliver high-quality results with minimal effort. This phenomenon is occurring in large companies across the United States, often unnoticed by the young professionals' superiors.

For instance, an associate at one of the top US banks uses AI to complete his week's work in a day and a half, spending the rest of the week studying AI videos on YouTube. This associate is responsible for analyzing and tracking spreadsheets of the financial performance of numerous clients, performing these tasks repeatedly on a weekly and monthly basis. By using ChatGPT, he has automated many of his regular tasks, resulting in work that surpasses that of his peers in both quality and quantity. His superiors are pleased with his performance yet remain unaware of his AI "hack."

AI first individuals use AI daily for both professional and personal tasks. They adopt a growth mindset, exploring AI's capabilities and experimenting with new technology platforms. These individuals understand AI's potential for breaking out of time-held personal limitations, expanding beyond their previously traditional roles. For instance, an AI first accountant might also engage in design, or a communications professional might code in Python. All of this is possible only because these individuals were using AI on a daily basis and using it as an extension to their own previous professional and cognitive capabilities.

When a small group of AI first individuals collaborates, the quality of decision-making, speed, and output improves significantly, compounding over time. At an AI-driven marketing firm, a team of AI first innovators transformed their company's digital-advertising strategy. Using AI-powered insights, they analyzed customer data swiftly and segmented customers in unprecedented ways. During a brainstorming session, an AI-generated report identified emerging trends, which the team immediately incorporated into their strategy. This agile approach led to a 20 percent increase in customer acquisition within a week. As time progressed, their decisions became sharper, their execution quicker, and their results more impactful. The campaign set a new industry standard, showcasing the transformative power of AI first collaboration. We've seen similar productivity gains at other AI first organizations we've worked with, and will provide additional examples of these transformations in this and future chapters.

AI allows businesses to scale operations rapidly and efficiently. For instance, AI-driven chatbots handle customer-service inquiries 24/7, while machine-learning algorithms quickly analyze vast data to identify trends and opportunities. An AI first mindset anticipates future trends and integrates AI proactively to stay ahead, rather than merely reacting to changes.

Just as individuals move from literacy to proficiency and then fluency in their use of AI, organizations follow a similar progression. Table 5-1 summarizes this progression. Initially, individuals might use AI as a Google replacement for search, then advance to drafting emails and blogs, and eventually utilize sophisticated applications like custom GPTs for specific tasks—for example, creating custom games to help children learn math. Similarly, organizations start by using AI for content creation and customer support, ensuring that new employees are proficient with one or more LLMs to boost productivity. AI first organizations, however, go further, by leveraging AI to innovate and create new business offerings. When C-suites employ

TABLE 5-1

Stages of AI first mindset in practice

Stage	Individual goals	Organization goals
Literacy	• Use AI for basic search and information retrieval. • Begin drafting simple emails and blogs with AI assistance.	Used primarily for simple cost cutting • Implement AI for basic content creation. • Use AI for customer support (e.g., bots). • Train employees to have base proficiency in AI tools for their individual use.
Proficiency	• Use AI for more-complex tasks such as custom GPTs for specific purposes (e.g., study aids, personal projects). • Develop custom AI applications (e.g., educational games for children).	Used primarily for workflow automation and ideation • Utilize AI for advanced content creation and detailed customer interaction. • Integrate AI into various departments to enhance productivity. • Ensure employees are adept at using multiple AI tools for different functions.
Fluency	• Innovate with AI to create unique solutions. • Use AI to enhance personal projects and productivity significantly. • Develop a deep understanding of AI capabilities and limitations.	Used primarily for strategy, margin improvement, and differentiation • Leverage AI for strategic decision-making and resource allocation. • Innovate new business offerings with AI. • Achieve significant impacts on business margins and market position through AI. • Cultivate a companywide AI first mindset, ensuring continuous growth and adaptation.

AI for strategic decision-making, resource allocation, and market positioning, they are advancing along the AI first spectrum. The real shift occurs when AI is used to make significant impacts on business margins or market position, leading to compounding benefits and a true AI first mindset.

The AI first approach requires continuous learning and adaptation. Teams need to experiment, learn from successes and failures, and stay ahead of technological advancements. Customer-centric innovation is key, with AI enhancing the understanding of customer needs through advanced data analytics and machine learning, leading to more-precise product development and marketing strategies. Strategic integration of AI involves automating routine tasks, enhancing decision-making with predictive analytics, and developing AI-driven products and services. Being AI first is about leveraging AI for transformative innovation and strategy, not just efficiency.

Adopting an AI first mindset involves a fundamental shift in thinking and working. For organizations, it requires changes in mindset and processes. Let's spend a moment comparing it to, and learning from, other types of mindset shifts that have been written about and celebrated in the past couple of decades. Many of our readers may be familiar with the "growth mindset" popularized by Carol Dweck, or the principles of "lean thinking" introduced by Eric Ries in *The Lean Startup*. These frameworks emphasize potential, development, iteration, and perseverance with an objective in mind. The AI first mindset is like these precursor mindset shifts and builds upon both of them. When you combine a growth mindset with lean thinking and add in generative AI—you get the foundation of an AI first mindset, which is foundational to realizing AI's full potential.

The growth mindset

The growth mindset revolves around the belief that abilities and intelligence can be developed through dedication and hard work. This contrasts with a fixed mindset, where individuals believe their abilities are static and unchangeable. People with a growth mindset embrace challenges, persist in the face of setbacks, see effort as a path to mastery, learn from criticism, and find lessons and inspiration in the success of others.

In a business context, a growth mindset fosters a culture of continuous learning and resilience. For example, when an individual or a team encounters a significant problem, those with a growth mindset will see it as an opportunity to innovate and improve, rather than a roadblock. This mindset encourages experimenting with new technologies, including AI, and integrating them into workflows to enhance productivity and innovation.

Lean thinking

Lean-startup methodology emphasizes creating continuous improvements and innovations by building products that customers want through iterative cycles of build, measure, and learn. Lean thinking starts with identifying the core problem that needs solving and developing a minimum viable product (MVP) to test hypotheses. Lean thinking is about reducing waste in processes, understanding customer needs through direct feedback, and pivoting strategies based on data and insights.

An example of lean thinking is Dropbox, which started with a simple demo video to gauge interest before developing the full product. By validating its concept with minimal resources, it efficiently directed its efforts toward building something that had proven demand. To achieve product-market fit, teams at Dropbox then went through a cycle of build-measure-learn with input from its target customers so features in the product and decisions about the product were customer-first.

AI first

An AI first mindset merges the adaptive, learning-focused approach of a growth mindset with the customer-centric, iterative processes of lean thinking, while also introducing unique aspects:

- Continuous learning and adaptation: Like the growth mindset, an AI first mindset requires a commitment to ongoing education about AI technologies and their potential applications. It encourages experimentation and learning from both successes and failures, ensuring that teams stay ahead of technological advancements.

- Customer-centric innovation: Like lean thinking, an AI first approach starts with the customer. AI can enhance understanding of customer needs through advanced data analytics and machine learning, providing deeper insights than traditional methods. This becomes even more powerful when synthetic personae and customer segments are used to provide feedback on products and marketing. This use of AI leads to more-precise product development and marketing strategies.

- Strategic integration of AI: An AI first mindset involves strategically integrating AI into all aspects of the business. This includes automating routine tasks, enhancing decision-making processes with predictive analytics, and developing AI-driven products and services. It's about leveraging AI not just for efficiency but for transformative innovation.

- Scalability and speed: AI allows businesses to scale operations rapidly and efficiently. For instance, AI-driven chatbots can handle customer service inquiries 24/7 providing instant support and personalized responses in multiple languages, and machine-learning algorithms can analyze vast amounts of data in seconds to uncover hidden trends and opportunities.

- Proactive transformation: While growth mindset and lean thinking encourage adaptation and responsiveness, an AI first mindset pushes for proactive transformation. This means anticipating future trends and integrating AI to stay ahead of the curve, rather than reacting to changes as they occur.

Implementing the AI First Playbook

With the right AI first mindset in place, a leader of an organization can take tactical steps to follow a playbook for implementing AI first action. The reason that a playbook is important in this context is the same as it is for a person wanting to be healthier or lose weight. The right mindset matters, but it takes more than just the right mindset to execute. Everyone needs tangible steps, ingredients, and frameworks to bring their mindset to action in the right way.

The playbook is for leaders who want to start the journey of transforming their company to becoming AI first, leaders of business units, teams, or companies.

This playbook, though adaptable to different organizational contexts, offers a structured approach to integrating AI:

- AI education and proficiency: Begin with comprehensive AI-education programs to build proficiency across the organization. These programs should cover AI basics, applications, and potential impacts on various business functions, providing hands-on experience with AI tools and technologies. The reason this is so important, and comes first, is that it is a precursor for the rest of the items in the playbook, and for proper governance and process for scaling AI within your company. For example, you can't effectively advise the company on an appropriate AI use policy or help prioritize potential AI pilots if you don't have a basic understanding of how the foundational AI systems work, what they are good at versus still needing to improve, or the variety of capabilities and work-flows that can stem from AI.

- **AI council:** Establish an AI council composed of cross-functional leaders to drive AI initiatives, ensuring alignment with business objectives and fostering a culture of innovation. The council should be composed of curious, passionate, and AI-literate functional leaders (or at least those committed to being educated in AI in real time while sitting on the council). It will be important to establish the council's leadership, roles, meeting cadence, communication protocols, mission, and purview. Having executive sponsorship is important, although the sponsor doesn't necessarily have to sit on the council. And it's important to involve IT and legal (and possibly procurement, if relevant) in the process, if not on the council itself, to ensure that the council is informed, not operating at cross-purposes with other existing AI-related activities and is positioned for success.

- **AI use policy:** Develop and implement an AI policy outlining ethical guidelines, data governance, and compliance measures, ensuring responsible AI usage. This policy should also empower teams to experiment confidently and responsibly, providing clear guidance on how AI can and can't be used, which tools are approved, and how to collaborate effectively with AI systems. The AI council can play a large role in creating and administering the AI use policy. Policies are usually seen as something that is restrictive by nature; but in this case, having an appropriately comprehensive AI use policy in place actually gives the organization *more* freedom to run pilots, experiment, and innovate without running afoul of smart security, privacy, ethical considerations, or other company efforts and approaches that could create a feeling of chaos or misalignment and ultimately slow down the desired transformational process.

- Road map and pilots: Create a detailed AI road map that includes pilot projects to test AI applications in various business areas, providing valuable insights and paving the way for broader AI adoption. The process of creating the right road map starts with auditing and discussing existing AI tools and projects, doing an assessment of the value and importance of a variety of potential AI use cases, ranging from cost savings to internal and external stakeholder-experience improvements, to unlocking revenue and product-growth initiatives. Only then can the AI council (or whomever is driving the AI road map and pilots) make an informed call on the best way to prioritize and administer which AI pilots should go forward.

- AI assessment and AGI-horizon process: Given the possibility that AGI or at least mid-level AGI capabilities are on the next-few-years horizon, it would be smart for companies and

AI councils to conduct regular assessments to evaluate progress and readiness for AGI. Implementing an AGI-horizon process to anticipate future developments and strategically plan for AGI integration is not just good future-proofing strategic thinking, it can also help with triangulating against what is possible (or almost possible) even given today's systems, which is a very helpful technique for road-map discussions.

Not every company will be able to, or want to, follow this playbook across its org from day one. As we will talk about later in this chapter, and throughout the balance of this book, every organization will have its own unique culture, business challenges, and internal capability to implement change, executive sponsorship, and pacing.

It's worth noting that while we have tangible experience doing digital transformation for large companies like Starbucks and Microsoft and relied on those experiences to develop this playbook, we want to give a shout-out to Paul Roetzer of the Marketing AI Institute who has been a thought leader in this space, teaching others (like us) about the importance of teaching companies to create a process that puts in place a foundation of AI literacy, competency, and governance.

Adaptability of the playbook

As referenced above, there isn't a one-size-fits-all approach to this. To transition into an AI first organization, companies need a structured yet flexible playbook. Companies vary in size, industry, technology adoption, proclivity, and leadership dynamics. Some leaders may aggressively push for an AI first culture, while others may prefer a more gradual approach, moving from crawl to walk to run. Some companies might benefit from a widespread, bottom-up, democratic approach to implementing the playbook; while others might benefit from a more top-down, lead-by-example, C-suite-led approach. The goal in any case is to achieve an AI first operational state as swiftly as is feasible for your context.

One example of a company that while not formally adopting each step of the AI first playbook we have laid out, nonetheless demonstrates clear executive sponsorship of an AI first mindset, combined with a lead-by-example top-down approach, is Suzy.

Case study: Suzy

We had the privilege of speaking with Matt Britton, CEO and founder of Suzy. We heard through mutual acquaintances that Britton had adopted an AI first mindset and was taking specific action to implement his own version of an AI first playbook, and that it was working well. As you will see, Britton took a more C-suite-led, top-down approach to becoming an AI first company.

Suzy, a consumer-insights platform founded in 2017 by Britton, has revolutionized the market-research industry. Britton, a seasoned entrepreneur with a background in digital marketing and consumer insights, had previously launched and sold several companies, including the social media marketing agency Mr. Youth (MRY) and the influencer content-creation platform Crowdtap. Recognizing the inefficiencies in traditional market-research methods, Britton aimed to create a platform that could deliver real-time consumer insights.

Suzy's core product offerings include Suzy Insights, Suzy Live, and Suzy Audiences, which provide large consumer brands with both quantitative and qualitative research. The platform boasts a network of over a million US consumers, delivering insights in days or even hours. Suzy's customers include major brands like Procter & Gamble, Google, and Microsoft, which use the platform for competitive analysis, product development, and consumer feedback. As of now, Suzy has grown to about three hundred employees and generates annual revenues estimated between $50 and $100 million.

Suzy's AI integrations: When ChatGPT launched in November 2022, Britton and his executives were eager to incorporate it into their product offerings. However, their enterprise customers were initially resistant, particularly their legal departments. While many entrepreneurial companies quickly adopted generative AI, Britton and his team at Suzy took a more cautious approach. For the first nine months of 2023, they focused on establishing a legal framework with their customers that would allow for AI integrations if and when the business units were ready. Britton worked iteratively and tirelessly to get a majority of his key customers to have their legal teams buy in with signed data-processing agreements in place.

Despite this progress, Britton still wondered whether the resistance was limited to the legal departments or if business owners were also hesitant. His strong sense was that the fear was widespread among his enterprise customers. Internally, Britton faced resistance from Suzy's legal, sales, and development teams. The legal department was hesitant to provide solutions, the sales team reported customer objections, and the developers were reluctant to explore AI's potential creatively. Britton's perspective on the AI market was that there was more talk than action.

As 2024 approached, Britton was dissatisfied with Suzy's progress in leveraging AI. He had a lightbulb moment: instead of figuring out an AI strategy, he decided to focus on the biggest issues facing Suzy's growth and see how AI could address them. He realized that AI should support a business strategy, not be the strategy itself.

This realization led Britton to a radical thought: could AI unlock his capacity to innovate and lead differently? Despite not being a developer, Britton dove into AI development, utilizing Gong's call transcripts and OpenAI's language model. He personally developed several AI applications that significantly enhanced customer insights and operational efficiency.

One of the first tools developed was the Churn Early Warning System, which analyzed customer interactions for signs of dissatisfaction and automatically alerted account managers to potential issues. Another significant tool was the Sales Training Application, which provided real-time feedback to sales representatives after each call, highlighting effective strategies and areas for improvement based on historical data. Additionally, the Call Summary Tool generated comprehensive summaries of customer calls, including sentiment analysis, key points discussed, and potential upsell opportunities, which were then disseminated to relevant sales teams.

Though we've simplified this to the essential details, it didn't happen overnight or smoothly. Over the course of the year, Britton systematically addressed resistance, which he categorized into three areas: legal, data security and privacy, and developer intimidation. He tackled legal challenges by prioritizing data security and privacy, ensuring compliance with data regulations, and gaining client trust through robust data-processing agreements. Recognizing that developers were initially intimidated by AI, Britton led by example, demonstrating AI's potential through tangible business wins.

The hard work of AI isn't always the technology; sometimes it's the service agreements, contracts, regulations, and ultimately, the people. Leaders often miss this, and an AI first mindset honors it.

By late 2023, Britton and his team had developed applications like the Churn Early Warning System and Sales Training Application. They viewed the failure of a deployment as learning rather than a reason to abandon AI. For Britton, there was plenty of learning but also success. Suzy's sales efficiency increased by between 30 percent and 40 percent. Additionally, the implementation of AI-driven tools allowed Suzy to maintain high-quality customer interactions and respond quickly to market needs, contributing to Suzy's ability to break even in early 2024 after significant losses the previous year.

Britton's success came from some deliberate decisions he made and from some serendipitous events. The three keys to his particular AI first mindset were:

- A top-down transformation: Britton's active involvement and his commitment to learning and applying AI technologies were crucial in overcoming resistance and driving the company's AI transformation. He led by example, building line-of-business applications himself and setting the standard for his team.

- Overcoming impediments and leading by example: Britton faced significant impediments, including resistance from Suzy's legal, sales, and development teams. The legal department was hesitant to provide solutions, focusing on the customers' fears rather than on finding ways to move forward. The sales team reported objections from buyers and saw impediments rather than opportunities. Developers were initially reluctant to dive into AI creatively. Recognizing these challenges, Britton took a hands-on approach, personally developing AI tools and demonstrating their potential through tangible business wins. This fostered a culture of innovation and continuous improvement within the organization.

- **Finding benefits in a remote organization:** During the Covid-19 pandemic, Suzy transitioned to a fully remote organization. This shift required the company to compile all Gong call transcripts and data into a centralized system. This proprietary data, consisting of simple customer calls and word documents, became a valuable resource that Britton used to develop AI applications. The remote setup ensured that all business information was accessible in the cloud, facilitating AI integration.

Suzy's transformation under Matt Britton's leadership is a compelling example of an AI first mindset in action. By overcoming initial resistance and focusing on strategic AI integration, Suzy significantly improved its operational efficiency and customer-insight capabilities. This case study highlights the importance of leadership in driving AI adoption and the transformative potential of AI in business operations.

The journey toward an AI first mindset is one of continuous learning, adaptation, and strategic action. By embracing this mindset, both individuals and organizations can position themselves at the forefront of the AI revolution, ready to capitalize on the immense potential of this transformative technology.

Chapter 6

EMBRACE AI, AND PIVOT HARD

At this juncture, a distinct point of view has emerged for us around how leaders should approach the broad, exciting—and sometimes scary—topic of how best to leverage AI in building their brand. It starts with an AI first mindset that will drive an organization toward implementing and scaling AI in its processes and product offerings. And when it comes to how a company should go about that implementation, we now clearly believe in the importance of laying a foundation around four elements, which proceed roughly in order:

- Establish AI education/training.

- Develop AI proficiency.

- Deploy AI governance.

- Run an AI opportunity assessment and road-mapping process.

As we covered in the last chapter, this foundational playbook has distinct elements, including:

- AI education and training, generalized to allow proper understanding of the capabilities, pitfalls, and momentum around generative AI, but with specific implementation examples prompting best practices

- Setting up an AI council

- Adopting an AI use policy

- Conducting AI impact assessment and AGI-horizon process

- Developing an AI road map and pilot process

But the breadth, speed, and sequence of adopting these elements will need to be somewhat fluid and customizable for each organization. As such, AI first leaders will have to adapt this approach and playbook to their own unique circumstances and culture.

Given how this AI first framework has crystallized, we have been moved to evangelize it to our "AI bootcamp" customers and our "fractional chief AI officer" clients at Forum3. Additionally, we are now eager and inspired to find as many real-world examples as we can of leaders who have taken some variation of this AI first approach—and discover what we all can learn from them. As such, we are going to round out the remainder of the book with a series of case studies and examples of different companies and organizations that have embraced some variation of this transformation.

In the book so far, we have organically seen examples of AI first initiatives emerge from Eric Vaughan at IgniteTech and GFI Software, Alicia Parker at Tishman Speyer, and Matt Britton at Suzy.

As you will recall, Eric Vaughan's approach to the AI first playbook was not only to adopt each of the elements all at once but also to require that *everyone* in his companies participate and share their ideas and progress. Eric's approach was to democratize the elements of the playbook, a horizontal, bottom-up approach.

On the other hand, Alicia Parker (as CMO) leaned in on behalf of her department only, adopting key elements of the playbook for her own team, as opposed to the whole company, and then shared out key learnings and best practices to the rest of the organization as she moved forward, a middle-out approach.

Finally, Matt Britton's approach at Suzy was to go top-down and adopt the right mindset for himself and his leadership team, and then go right into building a usable pilot that allowed him to demonstrate to his whole organization the power of an AI-based internal application.

And now we move to another amazing example: Sal Khan and Khan Academy. Khan Academy took a version of the top-down approach, similar to that of Suzy. But Khan and his team, because they were able to get a look at the power of generative AI at such an early stage, might actually have been the very first AI first organization out there, taking an approach that was fueled by a confluence of three key factors: the right mindset, a bias for action, and a history of leveraging technology to unlock their mission.

As part of our own ongoing AI education and research for this book, we had recently read the just-published book by Sal Khan, *Brave New Words: How AI Will Revolutionize Education (and Why That's a Good Thing)*. We were struck not only by Sal's innovative and forward-looking thoughts on the future of education, but by his own organization's story of AI adoption. It's hard to imagine an example of a company that was any quicker to take action integrating AI into its core products, and we wanted to understand how he did it and find out firsthand what that transformation process looked like, and what we could learn from it to pass on to you. His candor made this an invaluable contribution to filling out the AI first playbook.

Khan Academy, a nonprofit organization founded in 2008 by Salman (Sal) Khan, has long been at the forefront of leveraging technology to revolutionize education. With its mission to provide "free, world-class education for anyone, anywhere," the organization has consistently embraced innovative and tech-forward approaches to learning. Khan Academy has 265 employees and 165 million registered users worldwide. Ask anyone in the education or learning space, Who is the leader when it comes to online tutoring and self-paced learning tools? The first name that almost always comes up is Khan Academy.

Long before the public introduction of gen AI or ChatGPT, Khan Academy had been implementing its mission by leaning into the use of technology generally. The vast majority of Khan Academy's offerings prior to the emergence of gen AI centered around online videos, digital practice exercises, and a web-based personalized progress dashboard; all empowering students to learn at their own pace, in and out of the classroom. As Khan explained to us, "When I set up Khan Academy as a not-for-profit back in 2008, the only reason that I felt our mission statement was plausible was because I assumed that technology access and costs would keep coming down for everyone, everywhere."[1] Khan had been smart about projecting where technology would advance, and he baked that projection into his vision for Khan Academy.

So, prior to even seeing or thinking about AI in the specific form of ChatGPT toward the end of 2022, Khan Academy's leadership was already centering itself around the core idea of how emerging technology would be critical to fulfilling the organization's mission. Was AI part of that consideration set from the beginning? A little. But nothing like it is now.

Khan explains:

> I didn't think AI was going to advance as fast as it has. I imagined AI being part of it somehow. But the internet, on-demand video, software, all those trends, spoke to very low incremental marginal cost. And then we think about what world-class self-learning looks like. It always would have to be a form of personalized education, where the education caters to where you are, and what you need. With a mastery framework, if you haven't learned something well yet, you keep working on it. This is how, when you take piano lessons, or if you're an elite athlete, you practice your craft until you master it. But we didn't do that as a society with education, because we couldn't afford to do that for everyone prior to the internet. Already in 2008, I thought to myself, "wow, internet-based technology can really start to approximate that type of scaled personalization." And even then, I did not imagine what I would see in GPT-4 in summer 2022.

In the summer of 2022, before ChatGPT would capture the world's attention with its release later in the fall of that year, Khan had a pivotal experience that would set Khan Academy on an accelerated path toward AI integration. Because of Khan Academy's leadership position in the world of technology-enabled learning, Khan had made connections with top technology leaders around the globe, including those at OpenAI. He got early access to GPT-4, OpenAI's advanced language model that had not yet been released to the public. (As a side note, and as you'll recall, this was around the same time that Reid Hoffman was offered an early peek at and access to GPT-4 before the public release of GPT-3.5.)

This unique preview put Khan Academy in a precarious situation. Unlike most organizations that would later grapple with how to respond to new, powerful AI tools, Khan and his team were thrust into a world of possibilities without the benefit of established frameworks or industry best practices. Khan recalls the experience vividly: "This was four or five months before ChatGPT would even be released to the public, which you all know was based on ChatGPT-3.5, at least the initial public version. And when we were invited to those first meetings to see ChatGPT, I was kind of just curious. But as a person who follows technology, I was very skeptical of how far AI could have progressed."

Khan's skepticism quickly turned to amazement as he interacted with GPT-4. His first exposure to the magic of a powerful LLM was this private demonstration of GPT-4 by the OpenAI team. The model's ability to answer complex questions, generate new ones, and engage in nuanced dialogue was far beyond what he had anticipated. And it was all in the context of education—the context that mattered most to him. The first question the OpenAI team showed Khan was an AP biology question that ChatGPT was able to answer incredibly well. Amazed, and even a little confused, by how developed this technology seemed to be, Khan decided to test it a bit on his own. He wanted to see if GPT-4 understood the reasoning behind its answer, and he prodded the AI to explain itself, which it did without hesitation or mistake. (In another full-circle moment for this book, Khan mentioned to us that he later realized it was not a coincidence that the OpenAI team chose this particular AP biology question to show Sal, as it was the same AP biology Q&A demo that Bill Gates had seen and been amazed by earlier that week, as we covered earlier.)

"It was a holy-shit moment," Khan admits, echoing our own reaction verbatim. "After my first encounter with GPT-4, the OpenAI team gave us access to it—for the weekend—for myself, our chief learning officer, and our CTO. While it had some issues still at that early juncture, GPT-4 was far beyond where I thought the state of AI would be at this point in time."

It sparked an immediate urgency. Khan understood that this technology had the potential to fundamentally change education through scalable, personalized tutoring—the very field in which Khan Academy operated and the very mission it was founded upon.

Rather than waiting for a formal strategy or extensive planning, Khan decided to act quickly. He immediately thought that Khan Academy should build an AI-based tutor that could interact with students using natural language, in real time, as the students went through personalized learning journeys. It would be a form of a "pivot" from on-demand videos based on personalized courses to interacting and conversing ("chatting") with an AI tutor. His team had the same thought, and they collectively decided they needed to move fast.

This decision to act swiftly was driven by both opportunity and necessity. The opportunity was for AI to enhance Khan Academy's mission of providing personalized, high-quality education at scale in a profound way. The necessity was the existential threat that such technology could pose to his organization if Khan Academy didn't adapt quickly. "Even back then we realized that, while it may not be fully ready for prime time, it was pretty clear that it could very well be ready for prime time in the next two to five years, which is not a long time. So, if we don't really embrace this and pivot hard, we're going to be irrelevant."

It's important to remember that at the time there was no conceptual framework or pattern to follow to create an AI first organization, no broad-based scheme his organization could adapt. As Khan put it, "The term 'prompt engineer'—a term referring to extremely skilled ChatGPT users that emerged in the months following ChatGPT's launch—wasn't something that anyone had talked about yet." So, the matter facing his team wasn't some process or cultural or productivity question to tackle. It was simply having to take a raw look into a capability that could directly disrupt or propel his entire platform and organization. And his first reaction was to embrace it and get his team to embrace it. And that wasn't easy, and deserves highlighting as an example of executive sponsorship and leadership.

As Khan recalls:

> Within about two months of that initial OpenAI demo of GPT-4, we had about forty people on the team under a nondisclosure agreement so they could have access. And within about three months, we had the entire team under NDA with access. As far as I know, the only people in the world who really knew what was going on with GPT-4 at that time were our team, the OpenAI team, and the folks at Microsoft. Everyone who saw it at that time realized that "this is pretty powerful." But they definitely initially indexed more on the fear side of things.

This was especially relevant in the education market. Khan continued, "They were like, 'Hey, this thing makes up facts; this thing is not great at math; we're talking about under-eighteen users. How do we protect them? How do we moderate them, police them if they try to do shady things with it?' And the posture that I encouraged was: these are legitimate questions and fears, but let's just write all these things down and realize that they are just constraints or things that we design for, not reasons to not move forward."

This was a prime, and pioneering example of an AI first mindset, showing three of its key elements: learn and adapt continuously, be fast, and be proactive. Khan not only moved quickly in response to seeing the current state of LLMs and AI, but also correctly intuited that the AI technology would likely improve quickly. Khan's decision to proactively design a new AI-based personalized-tutoring product was based on this analysis—real AI first thinking.

The rapid adoption of AI at Khan Academy was fundamentally driven by a shift in mindset, particularly in the leader himself. This aligns with another core principle of the AI first approach we've discussed: Start by changing thinking at the leadership level. This allows for the right kind of executive sponsorship.

Sal's own mindset shift as a leader was characterized by several key elements that are worth calling out and reviewing:

- Openness to transformation: Despite initial scepticism going into the OpenAI demo meeting, Khan himself remained open to the possibility that AI could revolutionize education. He was able to trace a clear line from his initial thesis—that technology would be crucial for enabling personalized learning at scale—to the insight that GPT-4 could power an AI-based tutor platform, effectively extending and potentially accelerating his original idea.

- Sense of urgency: Recognizing the rapid pace of development, Khan felt compelled to act quickly rather than wait for perfect conditions. Because of his many years of personal experience in leveraging internet, video, and software technology to build Khan Academy, he was able to assess and predict the pace at which gen AI technology would likely progress from the first time he saw GPT-4. Having an innate sense of the pace of change allowed him to have the appropriate sense of urgency and bias for action.

- Balance of optimism and realism: While excited about AI's potential, Khan also acknowledged its current limitations and the need for responsible implementation. This was another great example of leadership that fits within the right AI first approach. Just because you are ready to move fast doesn't mean you don't need to have the right sense of boundaries, governance, and caution. As we've covered already in this book, we recommend that any AI first approach start with education and training; a smart AI use policy that considers security, privacy, and ethics; and governance and transparency through the right, educated AI council.

- Mission-driven focus: Every decision Khan made was filtered through the lens of Khan Academy's core mission, ensuring that AI adoption served the ultimate goal of providing free, world-class education. Making the decision to move fast wasn't driven by a desire to have a shiny object initiative to impress his board or the media; rather, it was motivated by a mission-driven need to see as many students and educators as possible be able to achieve their goals of personalized learning mastery.

If that could be accelerated and accentuated through a gen AI–powered platform, then Khan Academy needed to adopt that immediately.

. . .

We don't want to make this sound like magic. This mindset shift, however quickly it came to Khan and the leadership team, wasn't universally embraced across the organization, and it never will be in any organization. Khan faced the challenge all AI first leaders will: aligning his team with a new vision, even before there's a formal AI strategy in place.

Khan decided that using a show-don't-tell approach would be the best way to move toward alignment. Immediately after making the mindset-driven decision to move fast and pilot its own GPT-powered AI tutoring application, Khan Academy started building a basic version of an AI-powered personal tutor and teaching assistant, which it would call, "Khanmigo."

The first prototype was up and running within two weeks of Sal Khan's seeing the initial demo. Two weeks. That's how powerful this new technology is, and how much heavy lifting it can take on across a wide range of reasoning, ideation, and conversation; all critical traits for an AI-based tutor to have out of the gate.

Khan told us about the effect of moving fast and demonstrating the technology to the rest of the team: "I think once we were able to show the broader team—even with some of the basic prompting that we were doing back then—that we were able to do some fairly sophisticated things with the demo version of Khanmigo, it helped to motivate and align our broader team. We were even able to get the math to be far better than the raw model was capable of, and that was inspiring and helpful to getting the overall team more positive than they were on day one."

This is a key successful transformational practice to take note of. With new technology—particularly one that is potentially misunderstood, scary, or controversial—it can really help to just show the team what's possible, versus telling them or trying to persuade them. We saw this in the last chapter when discussing Suzy and its approach to getting the team to believe in the transformational power of gen AI. Remember, at Suzy, the CEO simply got to work building a first version of the sales-optimizing tech and immediately rolled it out to the team so they could experience the magic of it firsthand. Once they saw it, the objections and skepticism died down fairly quickly. It's hard to argue about theoretical negatives when you are witnessing real-world positives firsthand.

The same practice worked here with Khanmigo. Khan said, "I don't think that showing the early prototype of Khanmigo immediately won everyone over necessarily, but it definitely started building more momentum. And then, in the next couple of months, we had another hackathon, and I was definitely pushing folks to lean into it, telling them, 'Hey, we've got to do this responsibly, put on the guardrails, but let's move fast, because this window of opportunity we have is small. There's going to be a lot of people who are jumping into the space imminently.'"

. . .

Khan Academy's approach to AI integration serves as a reminder and an example of how not every company or organization will follow the exact same approach to being AI first. The more structured AI first playbook outlined in the previous chapter—as we have emphasized—needs to be adaptable and customized to the culture and situation of each company.

This playbook advocates for formal (somewhat sequenced) steps like first getting either a core team or the entire team educated and trained to an extent on AI, then establishing an AI council, followed by developing a comprehensive AI use policy, and ultimately creating a detailed road map. But Khan Academy's journey demonstrates the importance of the right mindset in any event, and also serves as a reminder that you can order these differently if the circumstances require. (Remember, no one was talking about councils, training, or use policies for gen AI in the summer of 2022, so it wasn't even a possibility to do this in any other order for Khan and his team.)

But now Khan Academy is moving quickly to get on top of many of the foundational elements of the more formal and sequenced playbook we have outlined, retroactively implementing elements that align more closely with the playbook. This evolution demonstrates the natural progression from an initial, agile response to a more structured, sustainable approach to AI integration.

Some examples of this evolution include:

AI education and training

- Khan is now actively working to educate his team about how to get the most out of AI, as well as about AI's potential and limitations. "I give these either weekly or biweekly video updates to the team. Little ten-minute videos were kind of what's front of mind for me, and I always try to make an example of how I use the tool myself so that people see that happening. And I hope this kind of encourages others."

Expanding everyday AI use

- Khan Academy has been exploring ways to better leverage AI in various departments' tasks. For instance, Khan mentions using AI for grant writing: "There was one example of where we're on a call with a funder and we had a whole email interchange back and forth. So now, I take the whole email thread and throw it into GPT-4 and ask it to write a first draft of a grant proposal for this funder, based on our email exchanges. Within seconds it provides a draft that the team can comment on and edit, and we can have something that is effective and ready to send within a day or so—a process that used to take a week or two."

- In addition, Khan has been pushing for AI integration in HR processes, such as analyzing employee surveys. As Khan explained, "One of my pet peeves has been that you do these company surveys and people write these verbatims . . . Now I'm just summarizing this with an AI. So I don't have to think that this is somehow the bias of someone in HR picking and choosing what they feel is important." Khan noted how this is both time-saving and gives higher-quality output.

- And when it comes to software engineering and coding, Khan was amazed by the productivity gains his programming team was seeing by utilizing AI tools such as Github Copilot. "I was shocked," Khan remarked. "A couple of months ago, I was just sitting at lunch asking a bunch of engineers about how much the copilot-type functionality has increased their productivity as engineers. There was consensus at the table that it was 3X—as in not thirty percent, but three hundred percent lift in output and speed because of gen AI. Three hundred percent!"

These examples show how Khan Academy is gradually moving toward a more comprehensive AI strategy, even as it continues to prioritize agility and innovation. As Sal Khan reflected on the improvements in productivity and quality the everyday use of AI is bringing to his team, he noted that "the biggest mistake in hindsight is that I wish I was even more aggressive in terms of the pace of our internal AI adoption in our everyday processes and decision-making."

. . .

Looking ahead, Khan has a clear vision for how AI will continue to transform education. He predicts significant changes in the next three to five years. For starters, he sees a shift away from traditional content delivery. As Khan put it, "I'm not sure if anyone's going to be using play-and-pause videos for anything. I think in the next two- to three-year timeframe, having a structured progression of well-vetted exercises, driven by natural language, voice-based (and GUI) interaction via all of these different AI supports, is going to be really valuable."

Khan also predicts that within a few years the entire self-learning and tutoring space will be dominated by very powerful AI systems, "A teacher is just going to say to the AI system, 'OK, you already know everything that the students have been doing, everything literally up till now, so let's create the right tutoring structure for each student.

What kind of problem sets do you think we should create? OK, now create it. Now administer it to the kids and keep me up to date."

Khan Academy's AI journey represents a unique point on the spectrum of AI first adoption. The organization's experience demonstrates that while a structured playbook can be valuable, the most crucial element in navigating the AI revolution is a forward-thinking mindset coupled with a willingness to take swift action.

As we've seen throughout this book, the AI landscape is evolving rapidly, and organizations must be prepared to adapt quickly. Khan Academy's story shows that sometimes the best way to prepare for the future is to start building it today. While not every organization will have the opportunity to be such early adopters, the lessons from Khan Academy's journey are universally applicable. By fostering an AI first mindset, being willing to experiment and learn, and always keeping their core mission in focus, organizations across all sectors can position themselves to thrive in an AI first way, in an AI-centric future.

Chapter 7

THE ESSENTIAL UTILITY

As we were talking to dozens of companies as research for this book—leading to, among other things, those case studies we have written about thus far—we kept thinking about Moderna, the small company that made one of the two primary Covid-19 vaccines. We were thinking about Moderna because OpenAI had published what it called a customer story about Moderna's organization-wide adoption of ChatGPT Enterprise.[1] The story was so in line with the AI first principles we've been developing, and the uses and thinking on AI were so compelling, that we kept saying, "If any leader had the same reaction to the Moderna/OpenAI story as we did, they would be tripping over themselves to implement a companywide AI transformation."

The story says that Moderna had put together a dedicated team of experts to drive a bespoke gen AI transformation program with a stated objective to achieve 100 percent companywide adoption and proficiency of ChatGPT Enterprise for all its knowledge workers within six months. That same team of experts had previously built an internal chatbot on top of OpenAI's API (which they called mChat) and launched a comprehensive change-management program including a companywide prompt contest as early as May 2023, which resulted in a large active internal AI champions group, 80 percent companywide adoption of mChat, and a 3,000-employee-strong AI forum. That initial momentum was perceived as instrumental in the speed with which ChatGPT was adopted when it replaced Moderna's homegrown client. Early adopters were using it more than one hundred times per week, creating hundreds of custom GPTs (AI agents) for specialized tasks. We couldn't have drawn up a better AI first model even if we made it up.

The customer story concluded that this transformation had taken hold and was producing results. Moderna's CEO, Stéphane Bancel, was quoted as saying, "We're looking at every business process—from legal, to research, to manufacturing, to commercial—and thinking about how to redesign them with AI."[2] As a result, according to the customer story, Moderna is able to achieve enhanced productivity overall, and thus help optimize its development and deployment of novel treatments with the same number of employees. "If we had to do it the old biopharmaceutical ways, we might need a hundred thousand people today," Bancel said in the report. "We really believe we can maximize our impact on patients with a few thousand people, using technology and AI to scale the company."

After all of the interviews with AI leaders and business leaders that led to our own AI first playbook, you can imagine our reaction to the Moderna customer story and these published facts. Immediately after reading this story, we started referencing it to all our clients at Forum3.

We would explain that, while we didn't have firsthand knowledge of the details of Moderna's AI-transformation agenda and implementation, it seemed to us to be the gold standard of the type of playbook we were starting to form from our own research. It became a staple of our presentations, yet we were only going off the short customer story that summarized what Moderna was up to.

We wanted the inside view of it, too, to learn exactly what led to this transformation program and the details of its implementation. We knew from reading the Moderna customer story that, in order to find out more, we'd have to connect with a specific and prominent character quoted in that story, Brice Challamel, Moderna's VP of AI products and platforms. Moderna agreed to let us have two long-form interviews with Challamel, and with his colleague Adrian Masson, Moderna's senior product manager for generative AI. Luckily for us, like so many of the other gracious interviewees in this book, Challamel and Masson were willing to help us learn in candid detail more about what led to Moderna's gen AI transformation initiative, how the company rolled it out, and what the implications have been thus far.

. . .

We found it fitting that Moderna, a company based on biological transformation, innovation, and technology, would be a leading case study on digital transformation in the AI age.

Most people know of Moderna as the company behind one of the most prevalent Covid-19 vaccines, Spikevax. This vaccine is recognized for its role in combating the Covid-19 pandemic by providing protection against the SARS-CoV-2 virus, which causes Covid-19. But it's worth spending a moment talking about the company behind the vaccine. After all, as in so many of the other case studies in this book, the Moderna AI first transformation agenda did not happen in a vacuum or as some bolt-on, shiny-object initiative. Rather, it sprang from leadership, culture, and mission, characteristics shared with many of the other early adopters of AI.

While Moderna was founded in 2010, its roots go back to mRNA research many decades before that. In 1961, several scientific papers identified messenger RNA, or mRNA, as the way that copies of genetic information go from the DNA in a cell nucleus to the outer part of a cell; and once there, the mRNA causes certain proteins to be produced. In the 1980s, scientists conducted experiments to see if you could prompt protein production by giving animals certain genetic materials. And it miraculously worked. Fast-forward to 2005, when researchers made great strides in proving that this could be done safely. And then in 2010, Harvard researcher and professor Derrick Rossi published a report detailing how his team had successfully used mRNA to transform skin cells into muscle cells without killing the underlying cells. That same year, Rossi, along with three other cofounders, created Moderna—shorthand for modified messenger RNA ("ModeRNA"). Moderna was founded on the research-based thesis that it could design an injectable synthetic mRNA that would cause humans to turn their own cells into protein makers, which, in turn, would prevent or possibly treat various diseases.

In 2011, Moderna's board brought on its first and current CEO, Stéphane Bancel. In the twelve years between Bancel coming on and the 2023 kickoff of Moderna's gen AI transformation initiative, Bancel and his team laid the groundwork for the business and culture of Moderna. Besides raising billions of dollars in financing, striking several landmark partnerships with the pharmaceutical industry, going public at the end of 2018, and going to market at warp speed with a groundbreaking Covid-19 vaccine, during those twelve years, Bancel created a culture of innovation at Moderna. He was known for creating an organizational focus on speed and throughput, all built on an overall company mission toward breakthrough innovation. The company's first and flagship product, while being a vaccine, was a form of innovative technology. In fact, Moderna's IPO filing documents showed a diagram flowing from DNA to mRNA to protein, and how it could be analogized to flowing from storage to software to applications, demonstrating how the company has always viewed itself as analogous to a software-platform company, in many ways more akin to Silicon Valley companies such as Apple or Google than to a typical biotech company.

Furthering its Silicon Valley platform mentality, in July of 2021 Moderna brought on Brice Challamel as a leader from Silicon Valley who was expected to help the company adopt an AI transformation agenda. This hire was before the world would be exposed to ChatGPT, which would be more than a year later.

. . .

From the very beginning, Moderna was one of many companies leveraging the cloud and investing in the general topic of AI-based transformation. Given Moderna CEO Bancel's mindset at the time, it's no wonder the company would be proactive around the topic of AI transformation. Bancel met Challamel during a learning expedition organized at Google's executive briefing center in 2019, when the latter was the global transformation lead for Google Cloud. It didn't take long before Moderna decided to hire Challamel to head up its own transformation efforts. Moderna felt it needed to improve its own ability to scale and be productive, and it needed a leader of Challamel caliber, with proven transformational experience and a playbook of his own.

At the time Moderna hired Challamel, the Cambridge, Massachusetts–based biotech was going through an explosion of growth in revenues, people, and product. It was no wonder. In May 2021 we were all still in the thick of the Covid-19 pandemic, with the total number of cases worldwide accumulating to astounding, seemingly never tapering numbers. By the end of May that year, the world had reported over 170 million Covid-19 cases, with the United States seeing over 32 million cases. But the trajectory of the pandemic had started to change around that same time. While cases were still technically rising, by May of that year there started to be a decline in new daily cases in the United States, with the average dropping under 30,000 per day for the first time since June 2020.

This decline and change in trajectory was attributed to increased vaccination rates, which were ramping up quickly. The Moderna Covid-19 vaccine began rolling out to the US population in large numbers following its emergency-use authorization by the FDA on December 18, 2020. By May 2021, Moderna had shipped over one hundred million doses to the US government, with more than sixty-seven million doses administered by that time, and forty to fifty million more doses being shipped per month. At this time, 57 percent of US adults had received at least one dose of a Covid-19 vaccine, with Moderna's vaccine being one of the key ones being administered.

The rapid distribution and administration of Moderna's vaccine during this period contributed to an explosive growth rate for the company. In 2021, Moderna reported sales of approximately $17.7 billion, driven by the mind-bendingly fast creation and rollout of its vaccine. The company expanded manufacturing capacity to meet demand, planning to produce between eight-hundred million and one billion doses in 2021, growing to three billion doses in 2022. This, all from a company that had *zero* product revenues prior to 2019.

It was in this moment—and with this backdrop—that Moderna brought Challamel on board with a simple mandate: always give Moderna a first-mover advantage. Clearly this meant that Challamel's mandate was to create the kind of conditions and culture at the company that would allow it to innovate more and move even faster, *and smarter*. This mandate can be traced back to the need for speed and throughput that Bancel had instilled in the company all the way back to 2011, and is part of a Moderna mindset that every employee learns when they join: act with urgency. At the time of Challamel's hiring, this wasn't just leadership jargon; the need was quite literal. If the company couldn't find ways to achieve a much more efficient, productive, and innovative working style, it could easily buckle under the need for resources or simply get bottle-necked in a crippling way. By the end of 2020, Moderna had grown to 1,300 employees, but still had way fewer people and resources compared with other biotech companies with a similar pipeline of unreleased products.

"When I joined in July 2021, it was the beginning of the Delta wave and a very critical time," Challamel recalls. "Moderna had around fifteen hundred employees, more or less, which was already big compared to what it was two years before, but small compared to what it is today. It was at the steep part of the S curve of explosive growth for the company, and a lot of things were straining under the pressure of hypergrowth."[3]

In Challamel, Moderna brought on a transformation expert. An *AI-transformation* expert, to be more specific, but a transformation expert nonetheless. Challamel had a background with and a passion for organizational culture and communication, and after a stint at BCG and running a transformation consultancy, publishing four books, and being a professor of innovation and transformation at HEC Paris, he joined Google Cloud in May 2016. While at Google, Challamel rose to lead the AI-transformation program, first working on internal AI-transformation enablement at Google, and ultimately leading the part of the company that would work with external organizations and companies on their AI-based transformation. On Challamel's team at Google was Adrian Masson, who would later join the team at Moderna.

"Working at Google on AI transformation, we met and worked with around four hundred organizations in the span of those three and a half years in which we were in the full swing of the first AI boom," Challamel explained. "The global C-suite transformation program spanned across all geographies, and all industries, with a focus in life science, retail, entertainment, and banking, which are data-intensive industries. Those experiences taught us a lot and were key to our ability to run transformation at Moderna. Our role was simply to drive transformation, but we did it four hundred times in a row."[4]

So when Challamel—joined by Adrian Masson and the head of customer engineering for the Americas at Google Cloud, Giraldo Hierro—started the process of driving transformational change at Moderna, he came equipped with a nearly perfectly suited skill set and all the right experiences for the task. And he had his own playbook for how to get started.

First step: go on a listening tour.

> The first thing that happened is that Stéphane invited me to interview everyone that I thought could be a component of the transformation capabilities of the company. I ran two hundred and seventy interviews with a methodology designed for this. It's something that I've done a lot in my life, and I know how to process, organize, and scale to reach a good outcome. I love the sentence "Listen before you think." It's hard because we think all the time. So we have to kind of shush our minds and try the best we can to become pure listeners with no preconception, simply wanting to understand what the person is about. And I ask a question at two thirds of the interview, which is always the same: "What would make you say that you have succeeded beyond your wildest expectations?"

Challamel explained that the answer to that question, especially when asked at that point in the interview, helps him anchor on the exact notion of ultimate success for that person, which would give him the internal drivers of 270 key people, of their organizations, of their work together, and give Challamel and his team a holistic and, as he put it, "a unique sense of awareness of the Moderna organization, where it stands, and what it wants to achieve—versus just reading job titles. If you really want to effectively transform an organization with this kind of growth and need to solve difficult challenges quickly, huddling together in the hallways in between meetings wasn't going to cut it anymore, not at that scale, size, and speed." From those first 270 meetings came a fundamental and somewhat basic discovery: Moderna had a major technology-infrastructure problem. And it wasn't something out of an MBA textbook or anything as complex or nuanced as you would think. "At that time, we couldn't always find a laptop when we needed one," Challamel remembered emphatically. "We couldn't always identify the owner of a process or a software. The company had been moving so fast on its core products, straining hard under pressure, it couldn't properly address basic IT needs. There were rooms at Moderna with no plugs to charge laptops. And I realized, if there's no electricity, there's no digital transformation."[5]

So, before even getting to the AI-transformation work he was hired to do, Challamel and his team were invited by Bancel to take on a sort of IT-transformation role. Even though Challamel didn't have any IT background, the company asked him to take on that foundational work. Once Brad Miller (the company's current CIO, himself a legendary tech figure who designed and launched the e-commerce platform at Amazon) arrived on the scene, he immediately saw the potential and moved things around to unleash the capability that he saw in them. Challamel, Masson, and the small but mighty AI-transformation team could finally start tackling the visionary work of finding the best way for Moderna to harness AI to unlock productivity, speed, and innovation as a first mover in AI first transformation.

This is an important point for anyone who is reading this book and is ready to dive headfirst into their own AI first transformation. You need to take stock of the foundational elements in your company that will need to be in place to get started. Everything from the very basic technology foundation of your people having the right computers and internet access, to thinking through who in your organization you would want to be a part of the training process, the communication of a rollout, the provisioning of enterprise-AI accounts, and the project management associated with a change-management program such as an AI first transformation agenda. We have seen examples of CEOs just taking the reins and leading by showing, but our best case studies in this book thus far involve a level of foundational and organizational prep; Moderna is clearly one example of this, but reflect back on how Sal Khan made sure to get his leadership team under NDAs in order to get early access to GPT-4 so they could be part of the Khanmigo prototype process.

. . .

At that juncture, Challamel, Masson, and team did what they do best, another listening tour. But this time they put slightly different ears on. Once again, they decided to focus on their people and run a set of 150 interviews across all departments—from entry level to senior leader—to really try to understand what problems might best be solved with AI. They were listening for clues to questions along the lines of:

- What would be the unlock to allow Moderna to have the kind of productivity, throughput, and innovation to deal with the weight of all of those pending products in the pipeline?

- How would Moderna continue to move fast and innovate?

- What kind of cultural or process issues was their organization facing that an AI-transformation agenda could help uncover and improve?

But they didn't start with the AI technology itself in mind. Challamel recalls, "We were trying to understand the problem from an AI standpoint eventually, but also and perhaps primarily from a data standpoint. We don't want to restrain it solely to AI, because it would have really just locked us in a specific domain. The AI technology itself will never be as good as the type of data that you actually have behind it. And so we really wanted to make sure the data topic was addressed in the discovery interviews."

This second listening tour happened at the beginning of 2023. At this very moment in time, OpenAI had just released ChatGPT to the world, which caught Challamel's full attention. He and his team immediately understood that what they were seeing was nothing short of the kind of technology that would bring about an AI revolution and that they needed to jump on it as part of their process. And, remember, this amazing little team at Moderna wasn't just your run-of-the-mill strategy or transformation team, this was a hand-picked team recruited specifically to leverage AI. The launch of a natural-language chatbot that could fully harness the latest transformer-based model and system couldn't have come at a better time for Challamel and team.

Challamel had studied every major technology revolution that came before ChatGPT and gen AI. They all followed a similar pattern, he pointed out. The new technology would come out and then be around for a while before eventually leading to a major democratizing application that, in turn, would lead to a revolution. This was also true of gen AI, as Challamel expounded:

> AI itself is not a technology revolution. The technology has been there for a while. But transformer models and gen AI, now that's a democratization revolution. The same happened for computers. The Turing machine came out in 1936, but it

wasn't until personal computing and PCs, in 1979, that we saw mainstream adoption. Same with the internet: it technically first came on the scene in 1969 with Arpanet, but wasn't mainstream until we saw the browser and the World Wide Web explode in 1996. There are waves and waves of these technologies that remain for decades in the hands of experts. They're hard to build; they're hard to use; and then, at some point, something happens and tips them over to becoming mainstream.

Challamel knew that he was seeing that moment here for AI with the release of ChatGPT:

> The moment when I realized that this was this exact type of transformation for gen AI was when Bill Gates was quoted as saying that ChatGPT was the most impressive technology he'd seen since the graphic interface. And the graphic interface was what democratized computers, because now you had a mouse and you could point and click and operate object languages. And so I thought, wow, if Bill Gates equates those two things, then we're at that tipping point for AI.

We smiled when Challamel said that. It turns out that for this book, the story of Bill Gates seeing ChatGPT, and his reaction to it and comparison to the first time he saw a GUI interface, is a somewhat cosmic, small-world moment for AI—as we have covered this exact same reference in the prior chapters that included Gates himself telling us the story, along with Reid Hoffman, Jaime Teevan, and Sal Khan.

So Challamel and team, following on their hundreds of interviews (for the second time), and after having seen ChatGPT and hearing the (now) soon-to-be-famous Bill Gates story, got to work.

. . .

It's worth pausing and noting that the first thing Challamel and his team did was to reach a conclusion and make a strategic decision about gen AI. They did this before any actions, communications, or initiatives relating to AI had started. The conclusion they reached was that gen AI would be a democratized technology that, if readily adopted by everyone in their company, would give the company the kind of productivity and innovation edge it wanted and needed. They likened it to the type of productivity, collaboration, and innovation unlock that had been seen previously by such technologies as the PC and the internet itself. This is a great example of an AI first–mindset principle in action: *have conviction and understanding around the power of gen AI, and move fast.*

Challamel concluded and advised the C-suite at Moderna that they should devise an AI-transformation initiative that would embed an AI first mindset and capability across all aspects of the organization and allow the company to achieve a step change in throughput and productivity. The company needed this, it was his mandate, and the technology was there for this to happen. In Challamel's mind, AI had the potential to augment the work and output of Moderna in such a way that the team could achieve the same output as a much larger number of workers. And this was particularly important for Moderna, given the explosive growth of need for the company's product at a time when there was no way Moderna could hire people fast enough to keep up.

Steve Jobs famously analogized the personal computer as being like the "bicycle of the mind." A human riding a bicycle can achieve going so much faster and farther using their own internal energy, sort of transforming into a different animal; one that can suddenly use their own power to go at speeds and distances normally only possible by horses, birds, and other species. The computer had the same effect on the mind of a human. And Challamel and team could see a similar speed and productivity transformational potential for an organization if it adopted gen AI writ large and in the right way.

So the team started devising how to do this using all of the principles that Challamel had studied, written about, and executed, both in his consultancy and professorship days, and from his time leading an AI-based transformation at Google. What he learned from his previous experience is that you don't just go at it with a typical training program or lecture. You have to inject this kind of transformation into the culture of the company, and that is all about getting people to truly understand and believe how this will help them achieve their goals and the company's goals.

"So Masson and I have this model in mind for transformation," Challamel excitedly told us.

It starts with the "user" [our people] at the core. The Moderna employees are people who need to want to transform. And if the people want it, the people need to invest time into it. That's how we will know they want it. So for this, we use three building blocks: culture, business, and technology.

This is different from what you usually hear, which is "people, process, and technology," because I'm not an HR person. I'm a transformation person. I need to change culture, not people, to drive behaviors that lead to business value. In the end, it needs to be something that's business critical for the users and that turns their dream of what they want to accomplish into reality. It's not about processes. I'm not an IT person anymore either. I'm not here to establish processes. I'm here to drive culture, to drive business on top of technology. And then you put a bar on this, which we will call governance because if you scale efficiently, if you succeed, you're going to need rules of engagement for all that ecosystem going into explosive growth, which is the case right now. You need to have guardrails and to have boundaries that are going to enable us to scale safely. But the first thing we do is put people at the core.

Let's summarize what Challamel is saying above, and relate it to some of the lessons we have learned earlier in this book.

- Challamel's transformation methods are rooted in the fact that you have to understand *why* you are seeking transformation in the first place. What are the key objectives of the company and each leader, and how will they best be served through an organizational or technology-driven transformation. What's working? What's broken? What traits and outcomes will have the most impact on the goals of each department and the company at large? In Moderna's case it was a need for productivity, throughput, and speed of decision-making and communication.

- Are there foundational challenges that need to be addressed first that are blocking the ability for broader change, and improvements that can be brought about by technology and process transformation? In Moderna's case, that was IT infrastructure.

- Once you see a major unlock from a technology—in this case ChatGPT—you need to get it into the whole company's hands in a way where everyone truly understands how it can help them achieve their goals, so much so that they *want* the technology, as opposed to feeling it's being thrust upon them.

So, how do you get the entire organization to both see and understand the revolutionary nature of gen AI in such a way that they will want to use it and invest the time to learn more about it?

You create a fun challenge that will appeal to the largest number of people.

For Moderna, its AI transformation started with a prompt contest. Yeah, a prompt contest. Sounds kind of nerdy, but it's brilliant and effective. Imagine a prompt challenge that resembles an Xprize contest that everyone in the company can take part in, with a CEO podcast kickoff and prizes for the winners. Challamel and team had in mind a contest that would be carefully put together and rolled out with just the right combination of executive sponsorship, gamification, fun, and technology.

Let's set the scene again. It's mid 2023. Challamel and team have been at Moderna for almost two years. At that time, over the prior six months, OpenAI had rolled out ChatGPT, and ChatGPT had already achieved the fastest user adoption of any technology in history, with over one hundred million users. But OpenAI hadn't rolled out ChatGPT Enterprise quite yet. The consumer-facing ChatGPT product that achieved so much traction wasn't as confidential as an enterprise API-based product would be, so Challamel and team needed to figure out which form of this new technology they would introduce to the full organization and how they would go about that.

They needed to solve for the form factor of the gen AI technology they would roll out, and at the same time solve for how to make it fun and engaging for everyone to see the revolutionary potential of the technology. For this, they reached out to Andrew Giessel, a seasoned engineer who had joined Moderna in 2016 and was a published researcher on applications of gen AI in life science as early as 2021, and would soon become head of AI engineering at Moderna. Giessel loved the idea and created for them an internal AI chatbot based on the ChatGPT APIs. That chatbot could do much of what ChatGPT's own website could do, but it would be confidential, secure, and include a number of custom features that would allow Challamel and team to track usage, make suggestions, and the like. They called this internal version of ChatGPT, "mChat."

They also needed a way of introducing mChat to the company, a way that would create that level of understanding and "pull" from the whole team, bringing about the desired effect.

First stop, the C-suite, which, including CEO Bancel, was put through a boot camp of sorts—to get up to speed on the specifics of ChatGPT and the power of the platform. Because Moderna already used AI in its core work, and had AI-proficient researchers as leaders in the company, the company had a leg up in being primed to grok just how profound ChatGPT could be if it worked at the simple natural-language prompt level. Once those in the C-suite had their own holy-shit moment and realized what we all now realize about ChatGPT and its capabilities, they got Bancel to dedicate an episode of his internal podcast to introducing and evangelizing to the entire company the revolutionary power of ChatGPT and gen AI. And this podcast ended with an invitation to register to use mChat and join a fun and massively rewarding companywide prompt contest.

But it's important to note that before kicking off the prompt contest, Challamel's team also reached out to David Porter, another important character in this story, whom Challamel had hired in his first months on IT transformation and who was a formidable tech evangelist with a long track record on digital education and literacy programs. Together, they made basic AI training and education available to the whole company via an online "AI academy" (which Porter now leads at Moderna) and organized precontest sessions and office hours. This is a key point that we have made earlier and throughout this book: AI training, education leading to a basic level of AI literacy, is the very first step that is an important unlock for the entire playbook. If someone has at least a basic understanding of how frontier AI systems and the underlying LLMs work, along with a foundational level of prompt lessons, they are much more likely to bring AI to the table every day and will start to see what it can and can't do, and will get the most out of it. We saw evidence of this earlier with the Harvard/BCG/Ethan Mollick research study, where the control group that also had a little bit of AI training saw the absolute best results.[6]

A lot of thought went into the prelaunch of the contest, as we just mentioned, from the launch podcast to the AI academy to the simultaneous launch of mChat, but great thought also went into the voting mechanism and reward system. Everyone would participate in this contest via the companywide Microsoft Teams chat platform, where each employee set up their own channel for submissions, voting, and communications. Every submission could easily be upvoted by others that liked it, and commented and built upon. And there would be three winners from each major reporting line of the company based on the most votes received from their peers. The prize? A trip for all of the winners to go to the West Coast and meet with the leading minds and companies working on gen AI, including OpenAI, Anthropic, and Microsoft.

With these elements in place, Challamel's team launched the prompt contest. They invited everyone in the company to join the company's internal Microsoft Teams channel and participate by submitting a prompt idea, and include the best parts of the chat/response from mChat. This would encourage Moderna employees from all departments to use the technology to show off their learnings in plain sight. This is another best practice from our playbook that we have talked about throughout this book: *The best way to learn what gen AI is capable of is to experiment with it and use it, and then share what you learned with your colleagues.* A prompt contest is a great way to achieve this and get people using AI in their everyday work, with an easy first step—a simple prompt and exchange with the AI to learn about the "jagged frontier" of what it's good at, what it's not quite good at, and what kinds of prompting techniques work best.

The contest went better than Challamel hoped. "At the time, the biggest Teams channel had ninety contributors," Challamel recalled. "So we opened this new Teams channel for the contest. We let everyone apply to it. And within a matter of a couple of months, we had three thousand active members on that Teams channel. That was basically the whole company at that point. We received more than four hundred prompt submissions, out of which we identified one hundred and eighty solid solutions that were game changers with gen AI on mChat. And to celebrate the winners, we published an article on our intranet with the title: '180 Things We Learned from You on AI.'"

Challamel's colleague, Adrian Masson, recognized that all of their interviews, IT foundational work, mChat creation, training, and education had started to pay off. "I think when we launched it, we expected to have probably one hundred submissions, and when we reached four hundred, it was way beyond what we could have possibly imagined," Masson recounted. "And this definitely relies on the hard work that had been done beforehand on making sure people understood what AI is through the AI academy, and encouraging people to follow the latest developments. So it was completely along the lines of one of our core mindsets to 'digitalize everywhere possible.' So it was one hundred percent within the mindset that we have."[7]

There was something viral and communal about the contest and the way it took off. It was designed in the lab to achieve this, so to speak. Masson continued,

> And so we could definitely see people just embracing it and going and sharing what they were doing with the tool. We were encouraging a way of thinking that we're very close to at Moderna, which is "yes and," encouraging people to build upon one another's ideas. And so when someone was submitting an idea, they had to submit the prompts, why it was helpful for them. And we were encouraging people to read this prompt, and "yes and" on how it could be better, how it could be improved.

Masson is touching upon a key reason the prompt contest was such a successful way to launch this effort at Moderna. It was *not* launched as a one-off training and pushed on the organization. Masson's team made efforts to have the core substance of the contest relate to real-world problems the various departments at the company were trying to solve. They did it in a way that encouraged interaction. And it was built on real-world prompting training and AI education that would benefit everyone as they continued to use this new, amazing tool at work as part of a transformation effort that would ultimately pay off in terms of productivity and innovation.

"I think one key thing that made this successful was timing," Challamel said. "The fact that this competition was not held in isolation. It was launched simultaneously with mChat as a new product, making gen AI available within the organization. And so there was this sort of celebration of being able to embrace it. And it became part of the culture with its name mChat, which meant "Moderna chat," and being the Moderna way of working." And he emphasized how important the AI training and education was as a foundation element to making this work:

> Alongside of this, we did develop some trainings available on a self-serve basis, where we were simplifying concepts so people could rapidly grasp what was going on, bringing frameworks for people to understand the types of use cases that they're exploring. One very simple framework that we brought in very early was to say, "Be careful, do not confuse this prompt box with a search box." It's a fundamentally new way of working, and you now need to give instructions for very specific tasks that need to be executed. And we started introducing prompt structures on the different components that you need to include within your prompts that really helped people.

And in order to sort through all of the submissions, votes, comments, and additions to the contest, they used mChat's inherent gen

AI capabilities and then reported out to the team what was happening. This again is another theme we have touched on in prior case studies: *use AI not just for substance but for business transformation itself.* AI is both the tool and the guide to making the tool ubiquitous and effective. "So we used mChat to just organize the reception of all those propositions and operate the whole initiative," said Challamel. "Otherwise we would have just exploded in flight under that number of people in that timeline. And when we realized this, we made this funny post called, 'AI for AI,' in which we explained how there's no way to organize this contest on mChat without using mChat."

It's worth calling out that by sorting through the most popular prompt submissions in the contest (as up-voted by the whole company participating), and then using AI to summarize and categorize the best learnings and opportunities for the company to leverage AI, Moderna ended up creating a natural AI impact assessment and early road map from the contest itself. We highlighted this in earlier chapters as a key step in the playbook we recommend for AI adoption. Here we see an interesting way for that assessment to happen as a downstream outcome of a fun prompt contest and companywide initiative.

Another notable outcome: the contest allowed for a natural way to create an AI council, something AI first organizations must do. The level of participation and energy for the contest created a kind of self-selection for such a council. You see, from the one contest and participation (submissions, votes, winners), Challamel's team could accomplish several good outcomes. They could see who was most passionate, proficient, and active at using mChat, both on the submission side and on the commenting side. This naturally would form the nucleus of an AI council of sorts, which they called the Gen AI Champions Team (GACT). As Challamel explained,

> The contest mechanism is to be up-voted by your peers, by people. So that allowed us to know who our champions were going to be. Because if you're good at finding a great prompt and you're popular so people want to vote for you, then you're good, you're popular, you're our champion. We're going to ask you to join us in the propagation. So that's how we identified our first hundred AI champions in the company. And of course, people voting for each other created a huge momentum effect.

As we have touched on throughout the book, having an AI council full of the right cross-functional group of employees/leaders that have had the right amount of AI training and proficiency gives the organization an ongoing way of creating, modifying, and overseeing an AI use policy, evaluating or piloting new AI products/features, maintaining momentum, and evangelizing the overall AI transformation agenda and vision. Normally we see an AI council being approximately four to eight people in the organization. But in this case, Moderna created a sort of mega AI council with its champions team, and the prompt-contest structure allowed it to have a natural and easy way to discover and have self-selection for the GACT from the entire company.

. . .

After the prompt contest and the formation of the GACT, this champions team became the primary mechanism for the continuation of the AI first transformation effort at Moderna. The team would meet twice per month, and they would have 60 percent to 70 percent attendance at every meeting. And that was saying something. The GACT was made up of over a hundred people, which were all of the most proficient and engaged employees that participated in the contest, and with natural attrition and self-selection.

The GACT was somewhat self-governed. Challamel likens it to guilds in the video-game community World of Warcraft. "I learned this from gaming, right? They were self-organized, so they elected their own leaders. They created their own groups. They have their guilds. They have their guild leaders. I don't interfere. Sometimes we're going to slightly nudge if we think a leader is challenged. We're going to help them. If we think there's relationship issues in one of the groups, we're going to just open it a little bit and support. But we're very hands off on the way that GACT self organizes."

And besides the GACT itself and its Teams channel, posts, and biweekly meetings, Challamel and his team conceived of and designed an incredible additional tool called Stardust. This was an AI-based agent that they created to privately evaluate and provide personalized coaching for employees using mChat based on their prompts, with no human scrutiny or intervention other than the agent's initial instructions. Stardust would autonomously send each employee a weekly email that recommended next best actions and prompt suggestions, and could even connect them with other employees that it thought were using mChat in similar ways—the idea being that they all could benefit from sharing their experiences and learning from one another.

At some point in the months after the launch of the contest and of mChat, GACT, and Stardust, the company moved from mChat being the chatbot everyone used to simply using OpenAI's ChatGPT Enterprise website. At the end of 2023, ChatGPT came out with a variety of improvements to its enterprise offerings, including web browsing, the ability to create custom GPTs, and a whole host of system-prompt improvements and multimodal tools. It became clear to the Moderna team that they should think of mChat as a way of working, and the literal tools could be left to the major AI system players like OpenAI. So after some deliberation around the question of internal-tool mChat versus off-the-shelf ChatGPT Enterprise, as well as the question of how many employees should get access to ChatGPT Enterprise, they decided to go all in. They bought Enterprise licenses for all knowledge workers in the company, and encouraged its use as stewarded centrally through the GACT.

And use took off (see figure 7-1). Challamel recalls:

> First there was an mChat era, and then we acquired ChatGPT Enterprise licenses, which is so much more capable because of all the capabilities built in: web browsing, coding, image generation, and so on. And that's when we really started to push for adoption and proficiency much more heavily than before, because until then we were more exploring and leveraging goodwill. And then we're like, all right, this is real. We need to get through this in the numbers. And that's something I think that would be of interest to you, because we are very data driven and constantly monitored and documented the progression.

. . .

At the time of our interviews with Moderna's AI leaders, it had been approximately nine months since the conclusion of the prompt

FIGURE 7-1

ChatGPT Enterprise adoption at Moderna

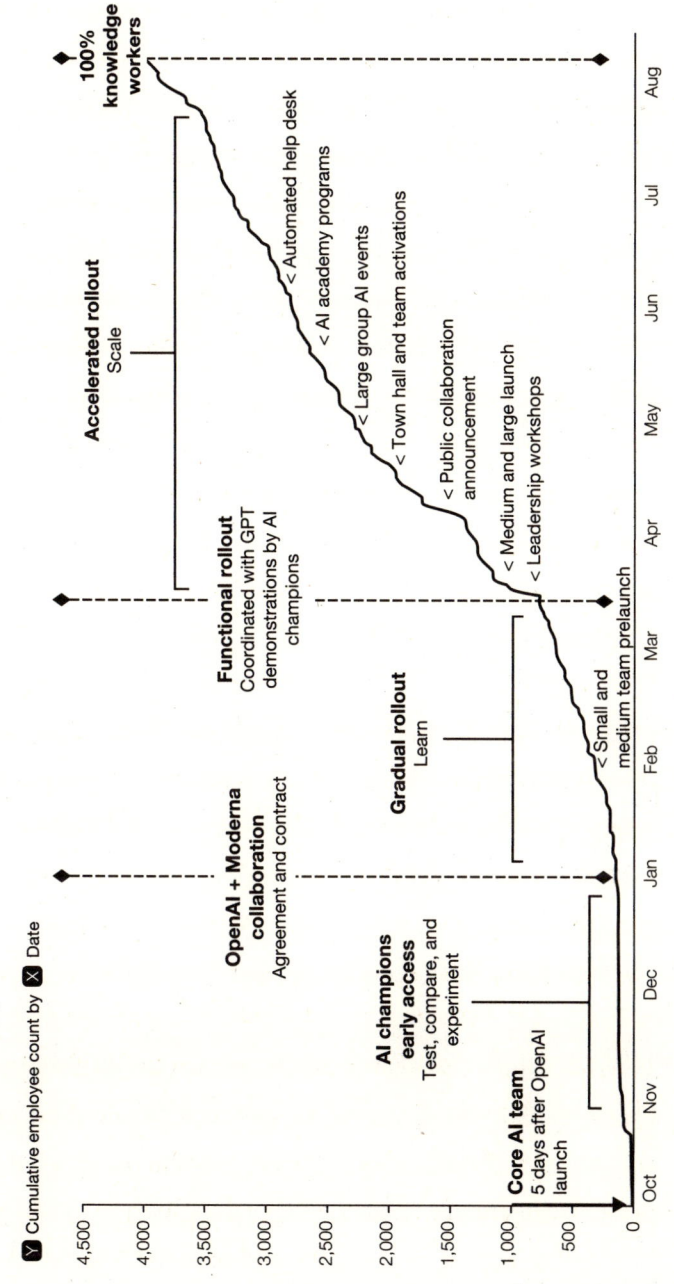

Source: Adapted from a chart provided by Moderna, 2024.

contest, the formation of their gen AI champions team (GACT), the winners' trip to the West Coast, and the launch of Moderna's AI first transformation.

We knew from the OpenAI customer story that this launch continued to have a profound, transformative impact on the company in terms of productivity, knowledge sharing, innovation, and communication. But we wanted to dig deeper. After all, we had the opportunity not only to learn about the mechanics and details of a successful AI first transformation process but also to do so from a team of world-class transformation experts. So we dug in on questions relating to their thinking of *why* they set up this process the way they did, and *why* they thought it would take hold the way it did.

When we started asking these questions, the first thing Challamel brought up were OKRs. OKR stands for "objectives and key results." It is a goal-setting framework that helps organizations and individuals track their progress toward achieving their goals. Objectives are clear, aspirational goals that define what you want to achieve. And key results are specific, measurable outcomes that indicate progress toward achieving those objectives. OKRs help to ensure that everyone in an organization is working toward the same goal, with clear priorities.

Remember all those interviews that Challamel and team held before even conceiving of the prompt contest? As Challamel recounts,

> The first thing is we work with OKRs, Adrian [Masson] and
> I, even though this is something we learned to do at Google,
> and we set early objectives and key results to match against
> those. We challenge ourselves very much. We share this with
> our leaders, and we make sure we align with those. So we are
> very driven by the OKR structure in everything that we do.

And still to this day, right from day one and to this day, we have four pillars of OKRs: strategy, governance, road map, and transformation. So strategy is what it seems like. How are we thinking about this? Where are we going? What are we trying to achieve? Governance is, How do we organize this to scale efficiently and safely? Road map is about consolidation, and transformation is about expansion.

Challamel explained that they took some of the inspiration for this from the famous AlphaGo project and Go game principles, which we covered in chapter 4. In the game of Go, there are so many different permutations and possible board positions that in some ways it mimics the vast and dynamic combinations of trying to achieve a result in the real world of life or business. In the game of Go, the number of legal board positions is estimated to be around 2.1×10^{170}, which is greater than the number of atoms in the observable universe. This makes Go literally a googol times more complex and varied than the game of chess.

Challamel talked about how trying to accomplish a successful transformational project is more like playing Go than playing chess. "We operate with Go game principles. This is not a chess match in which you're either defeating someone or being beaten yourself," he said. "This is more like a territory-building exercise. And I find that rooting this in Go game principles like 'expanding territory, understanding territory, and branching out' speaks more to our imagination. So we're constantly asking ourselves, What can we consolidate and where should we expand?"

So what are the vital behaviors that need to evolve for the Go game to accomplish its purpose and create a new type of territory, in this case transforming a corporate culture to be ready for the age of generative AI? According to Challamel they are:

- Be data driven

- Participate and learn (growth mindset)

- Collaborate and share

- Innovate and experiment

- Integrate AI into your business

- Measure and track your progress

. . .

Moderna's implementation on an AI first transformation was anything but a rushed, check-the-box play for the company. It was born of a culture rooted in technology-driven transformation and innovation. It was carefully planned by a group of leaders who had specialty experience and talent in the very domain of AI-based transformation, and who deeply understood the technology and its potential. And it was executed with a variety of best practices, from executive leadership to training/education to companywide participatory exercises that encouraged learning by doing in a practical context.

So, we were eager to ask the questions: "Has it worked? How do the company leaders think or talk about their AI transformation efforts in terms of ROI?"

On the topic of ROI, the first thing that caught our attention from the original Moderna customer story on OpenAI's website was how Moderna's CEO, Stéphane Bancel, pointed out that the company's AI first transformation implementation is allowing Moderna to operate with the same five thousand people in a manner akin to that of a much larger organization. In other words, this transformation had the effect of allowing Moderna to scale up its productivity and capacity. Instead of using this productivity gain to reduce its costs, it kept the same cost structure and grew throughput and output at a large rate. If even directionally accurate, this would point to a massive ROI on the time, effort, and cost the company put into conceiving of and rolling out an AI first transformation program.

When we asked Challamel about Bancel's observation and the topic of ROI, he said he first wanted to get something off his chest:

> If I'm honest, when I see that some people doubt the efficiency of the usefulness of gen AI, I feel that we [at Moderna] must live in another world, because Moderna is concrete proof of it every day, ten times a day. So I don't understand. I am probably on the other side of the "trough of disillusionment" of the hype cycle, and others are still behind us going down the slides, but I'm seeing them from the distance, from the other side of the chasm, and I just don't get it. I think to myself: Why would you be so doubtful when there's so much that is already being delivered and done staring you in the face?

Challamel is referring to the famous hype-cycle image, which shows it going up, then down, then back up again on the other side (see figure 7-2).

At some point the company was seeing so much overall progress in terms of productivity, throughput, innovation, and outcomes stemming from this AI first transformation that it stopped talking

FIGURE 7-2

Gartner hype cycle

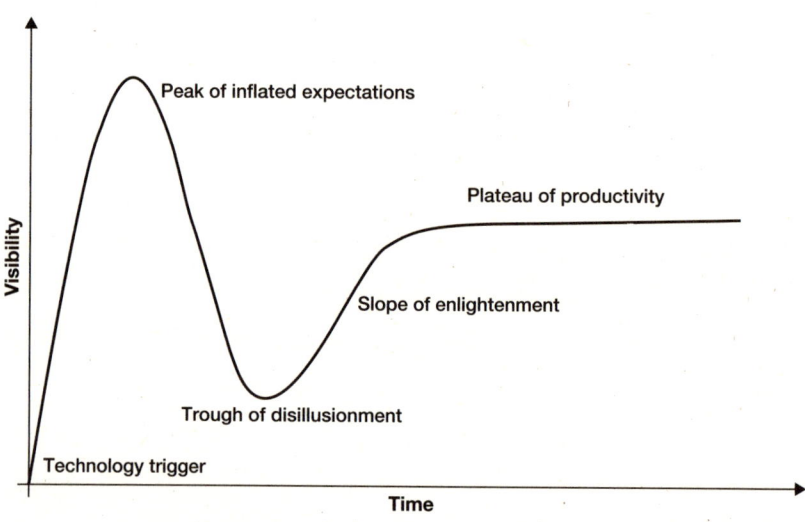

Source: Jeremy Kemp/Gartner Research, 2007.

about it in terms of traditional ROI. When we asked about when that happened, or how the company convinced internal sceptics, Challamel replied,

> What's complicated here is that on a task-by-task basis, your efficiency gains are through the roof. You can go from five hours to ten minutes on some of them, but you don't do them every day, ten times a day, either. So you have to both understand the profound impact on the daily-task-based items, but also how that plays down in the long tail of the company. So that's why, with Stéphane's approval, we didn't overemphasize the calculation of return investment on this technology. No one ever gave me the ROI of electricity at Moderna or the ROI of

laptops at Moderna. I don't know those numbers, and I don't think anyone calculates them. And I think highly enough of gen AI that I believe it's in the same category.

This point is a crucial point to focus on. So many leaders right now read about the "power of generative AI" and hear the hype over AI in the news every day, and their first reaction is to want to jump right into the process of building or enacting some big new AI initiative that will save a bunch of costs, or drive more sales, all driven from this big-bang new AI idea that they hope someone will help them come up with. And while that is absolutely a fair way to think about the potential of this new technology, it also misses the larger point right in front of them. This technology is not like prior technologies, even though it builds upon them. The immediate power of generative AI is that it is a nearly free source of general-purpose "intelligence as a service." It's more akin to having access to white-collar or knowledge workers on demand. It's about a new way of working and making decisions, and even collaborating. The first and most powerful opportunity for most companies is to integrate this intelligence into their daily tasks, decisions, and processes to gain a double-digit percentage of productivity—a productivity boost that shows up both quantitatively and qualitatively. And from there, their own teams can start to assess, ideate, and experiment with the big-bang ideas for major boosts in customer experience, sales, and expense structures. This everyday and always-on benefit of an organization using generative AI as a cointelligence tool is what Challamel was pointing out above when he compared asking about the ROI on a fully deployed AI transformation with asking about the ROI on computers or electricity.

We asked Challamel what his advice would be for executives just starting out on their own AI-transformation journey. He had two pieces of advice: Don't oversell genAI, and believe in your people.

> Gen AI is so amazing and making so much progress that we can forget at times to remain both curious about the latest capabilities, and cautious about the inherent limitations," Challamel said. "Transformation is not about technology but about people, and what matters the most is to augment them in a way that feels both inspiring and safe. Trust them to find how the technology can make a difference for them and for your organization and let them show you how awesome they are. This is how you can best help them go from heroes to superheroes in their life pursuits.

Near the end of our time together, Challamel made the following observation:

> You know, when you teach your children to bike and they think they can never figure out how to stay balanced? How could they? Because this thing, it keeps falling. It has no balance. You're asking them to do the impossible! But because you love them so much, because you believe in them so much, you know they're going to figure out how to ride a bike, and when they do, the pleasure you will get out of them doing this is bigger than the one you would have learning it for yourself.

. . .

This was a lot, we know, but it's so full of useful guidance and practical takeaway that we didn't want to leave any of it out. To help organize your thinking on the best practices found in this case, here's a summary of how Moderna exhibited each of the AI first playbook items based on what we have learned in this book thus far:

1. AI education and training

   - Moderna's AI academy: To ensure widespread AI adoption, Moderna launched an internal AI academy, which provided training to employees on how to use AI, including basics like how to craft effective prompts for mChat.

   - Precontest sessions and office hours: Before launching their AI-prompt contest, Moderna held sessions to train employees on how to use AI tools, fostering familiarity and increasing confidence in leveraging AI for their specific work processes.

2. Develop AI proficiency

   - Prompt contest to drive proficiency: Moderna encouraged employees to develop their AI skills by holding a company-wide prompt contest. This contest challenged teams to come up with useful AI prompts relevant to their roles, promoting hands-on learning and experimentation.

   - Usage metrics: Moderna tracked employee engagement with AI, measuring weekly usage (over one hundred times per user) and the creation of hundreds of custom GPTs, ensuring AI proficiency was deeply embedded in daily workflows.

3. Deploy AI governance

- **AI Champions Team:** Moderna established the Gen AI Champions Team (GACT), a group of more than a hundred proficient AI users who were selected based on their engagement in the prompt contest. This group not only supported AI usage but also helped set guidelines and best practices for the wider organization.

- **Guardrails for safe AI usage:** The leadership team, including Challamel, acknowledged the importance of implementing governance structures to ensure that AI was used safely and responsibly. This involved establishing clear rules and guidelines as AI usage grew.

4. Run AI impact assessment and road mapping

- **Prompt contest naturally led to AI assessment and road-map opportunity:** By starting with a prompt contest that had participation from across all functions and divisions of the company, and then organizing the top submissions using AI ("180 Things We Learned from You on AI"), the contest structure allowed for an organic, self-forming type of AI assessment and early road map.

- **Iterative approach:** Moderna used a road map to guide its AI integration, beginning with the infrastructure upgrades (like improving IT) and gradually moving toward more-advanced AI applications, such as internal chatbots and collaboration tools.

5. Executive leadership with an AI first mindset

- CEO Stéphane Bancel's AI commitment: Moderna's leadership, especially CEO Bancel, was deeply committed to the AI transformation. His emphasis on scaling the company using AI rather than human resources drove the entire transformation forward.

- Brice Challamel's visionary leadership: Challamel's experience with AI transformation at Google played a crucial role in aligning Moderna's leadership and employees around the AI first mission, with his listen-first methodology ensuring that transformation efforts addressed real employee needs.

- Strategic decision to embed AI: Moderna's leadership made a strategic decision early on to embed an AI first mindset into their organization. They didn't just experiment with AI tools—they deliberately aimed to use AI to create a significant productivity and innovation boost.

6. Show, don't tell

- Using mChat to showcase AI's power: Instead of relying on abstract discussions, Moderna showcased AI's capabilities by building mChat, an internal AI chatbot. The prompt contest further demonstrated how AI could directly improve employee workflows, leading to widespread engagement and understanding.

- AI for AI: Moderna used AI tools to sort through the more than four hundred contest submissions, showing employees how AI could not only solve problems but also streamline internal processes, further cementing AI as an indispensable tool.

7. Flexible and adaptable implementation

- Iterative rollout of AI: Moderna adapted its approach as needed, starting with basic IT infrastructure fixes, and then launching mChat and the prompt contest to engage employees. Over time, the company transitioned from mChat to OpenAI's ChatGPT Enterprise as the technology evolved.

- Adaptation of AI to business needs: Rather than enforcing a rigid structure, Moderna allowed its AI transformation to evolve organically. The company started with internal experimentation and, as AI use cases proved successful, rolled out more-formalized tools and governance structures across the organization.

Conclusion

ANOTHER INTELLIGENCE IN THE ROOM

As we write these final words for this book, we've been on our AI journey for a year. We have learned so much about this revolutionary new technology, and the framework that leaders and brand builders should adopt when confronting how best to embrace it, with those lessons coming to a sort of crescendo with the last chapter highlighting Moderna's AI first journey. It feels like a natural place to stop for now and reflect.

As we set out to write a sort of end cap to the book, we realize that our journey is just beginning, not ending. The lessons we learned, and the AI first playbook approach we have put together, are just an introduction to the next chapter in that journey. They are a means, not an end, to a new way of thinking about working, building, and innovating.

In that sense, this concluding chapter should circle back to where we started—with a beginner's mind asking broad questions and challenging ourselves to continue learning. Where does our AI first playbook go from here?

Maybe it's just because we needed to wrap up our writing on the book, or perhaps it's related to the fact that GPT-5 is rumored to be coming soon, but in our own research and experimentation, we can feel something brewing; that disquieting feeling you have that everything is about to speed up again. We can't help but notice the compounding effect of the frontier models getting smarter and more capable, adding multimodal tools, and the effects of the AI race involving OpenAI, Google, Microsoft, Amazon, Apple, Meta, xAI, and Anthropic getting ready to produce the next wave of holy-shit moments for us.

Recent examples include seeing OpenAI release its o1 model that can do chain-of-thought reasoning on its own and that has hit nearly PhD-level intelligence; Google's NotebookLM product that can instantly create a totally realistic two-person radio/podcast-style audio show based on anything you upload to it; Amazon recently touting that it used its own Q system to save 4,500 years' worth of engineering time (value: $250 million) on upgrading its own system from Java 11 to Java 17, taking something that would have required two months down to five days; and, finally, Apple's new iPhone 16, which just came out and will bring Apple's own AI systems to hundreds of millions of new iPhone users.

The AI first playbook from this book feels like the right foundational next step for any organization or brand to adopt, but we are asking ourselves—even challenging ourselves—to look at it from the perspective of someone reading this book a year from now. Does the playbook go far enough?

So we approached one of our AI gurus that we follow and learn from every day, Professor Ethan Mollick. We wanted to ask Professor Mollick to review the key elements of this book, and challenge them, build on them.

Professor Mollick isn't just one of *our* AI gurus. He plays that role for most people paying close attention to this space. Mollick is a prominent academic and thought leader in the fields of innovation, entrepreneurship, and of late, generative AI. He is currently a professor at the Wharton School (University of Pennsylvania). His research focuses on the effects of gen AI on work, entrepreneurship, and education. His work has been published in leading scholarly journals as well as the *New York Times* and CNN, and his latest bestselling book on the topic of gen AI is *Co-Intelligence*. He is a prolific writer and researcher on this topic and covers his thoughts and research on his Substack (*One Useful Thing*) as well as through his numerous speaking engagements and media appearances. If you want to truly wrap your head around what's possible, what's known, and what's unknown in the gen AI space, you follow Professor Mollick.

In our interview with Mollick, he immediately pointed out that "it was a good thing your book is being published serially and will come out relatively soon. Otherwise, by the time it comes out, many of its messages could be outdated."[1]

OK, that's a good start, we thought. But quickly he leaned into the camera and gave us what felt like a warning:

> Everything you're saying, you know, resonates with somebody
> who's written a book on this topic. Your playbook is great,
> but that wouldn't be the playbook I'd be writing for next year,
> right? I saw you write in your book about agents. Agents are not

far away. You know, we're close to the next level of reasoning from the frontier models. People aren't really thinking about full multimodality, which is another thing I saw that you mentioned, but with that, there's a whole shift that's coming. And there's not a single person, including all the people you talk to in this book, that when you interviewed them six months ago or eight months ago, they were a little more doubtful about how long the scaling law curve would last. I don't hear anyone saying that anymore. They all expect at least two generations of rapid increases from here.

His point was to remind us that AGI (or something close to it) is coming in a few years; and not to forget the profound implications of that on how leaders and organizations work and innovate. This is literally the point that this book started with—the Sam Altman interview and his focus on AGI. It was a good reminder. We saw ChatGPT for the first time just shy of two years ago, went on this research and writing journey a year ago, and have seen so many business leaders being still so far behind the curve when it comes to understanding and leveraging this technology. So we built a set of principles and a playbook that allow any company to come up to speed and get its own journey moving, but Mollick was reminding us not to take our eye off the ball that Sam Altman had pointed out was coming at us quickly; to make sure our advice and our playbook accommodate how fast-moving this space is.

Mollick points out that there are at least two huge turns of the crank coming, with GPT-5 and GPT-6 levels with better reasoning and more agentic capabilities. And they will likely swallow up "wrapper apps" (apps that are mostly just one of the frontier AI models' APIs wrapped in some basic UI and prompts) or even heavier-duty applied AI apps available today. As a result, you can't get complacent in just addressing and utilizing the technology as it exists today, and you can't just treat it like a new app or cloud service that becomes available to you. As Mollick put it, "I think people are getting used to the first wave of disruption, which is like, 'wow, this stuff does amazing things, like, you know, that you call the holy-shit moment. In my book, I talk about how I had three sleepless nights when I first saw it. And then most companies flub this by handing it off to IT and to the legal department first, and waste a year with it, building rag-based solutions that'll never really work or do the kinds of things they want."

Mollick's point here is that we should continually be emphasizing the size and the speed of the coming change. He pointed out to us that we should be much more emphatic to the readers of this book (and the companies we advise) that companies must have a dynamic mind-set in how they set up for these changes. In other words, the question should be not just about whether leaders are following the playbook to get the most out of this new technology but also about what the playbook is even for? "What I'm saying is that what's missing from your playbook is dynamism," Mollick admonished. "In your book, you're talking about case studies of leaders who made a stand now and want to build on [gen AI] as it exists today. But we are not used to a world where things are happening very quickly, and you have to take a stake on the future."

Mollick points out how most companies that are seeing this first big wave of gen AI are sort of complacent. Either they aren't doing anything at all—and are frozen like a deer in headlights, trying to make sense of what this new technology is and what it means—or they are doing something about it but are still being too passive. Mollick explained, "There's a huge gap. Out of any hundred companies or CEOs I talk to, one really gets it. Four have possibly useful projects underway, and the rest are disasters of various types. Right? The rest are waiting for McKinsey to tell them what to do. I'm fine. It's okay, right?" Mollick continued, "I kind of worry, the first adoption of 'copilots' kind of froze a bunch of organizations in place, because they got used to the copilot. Then they did not build their own stuff. They are frozen in place."

The natural question to ask, then, is What should they be doing if not at least trying to adopt and use the technology as it is today? We asked Mollick specifically: Beyond even using our AI first playbook, what else should companies be doing to exhibit the kind of dynamism and future proofing he is alluding to?

His answer: they should be building a gen AI R&D lab right now.

At first, and even during the time of the interview, we had a sort of cognitive dissonance with this answer. Quite literally, we stood quiet for a moment, and then remarked, "But we can barely get leaders to really take the time to do proper AI literacy training and adoption, and you want them to jump all the way to creating an AI research and development lab? In fact, some companies question the spend on getting all employees ChatGPT teams!"

Mollick didn't blink or miss a beat. He likened gen AI to Covid-19, and what happened during the shutdown and the years after:

> I know this is hard for organizations. And it does involve redoing things, but you cannot have organizations structured the same way. We can't pretend that there isn't another intelligence in the room right now. Think about what happened when

Covid shutdowns hit us. If you talked to any *Fortune* 1000 company and said, with one-day notice, everyone has to leave the office with no new technical systems, no clear guidance on how to work remotely, and you won't return to full office work for three years, every single company would have said, we're going to collapse. But not a single *Fortune* 5000 company collapsed. Obviously we have a lot of flexibility inside organizations we're not taking advantage of at all.

The Covid-19-shutdown and remote-work analogy struck us hard. There is a wave of AI capabilities and disruption that is coming fast— maybe as early as this year or the year after (2026)—and the ramifications of how it will change the way we work and build companies, organizations, and brands will be substantial; possibly as substantial as the changes that were forced upon us by the lockdowns and remote work. But Covid-19 showed that when pressed, we humans and businesses are able to make big changes quickly in the way we work, collaborate, and establish processes. It turns out that we have much more of an ability to adapt and to change the way we work than we think, and that power is latent within our organizations today.

We started to see what he was saying. There is "alien" intelligence that is already in the room with us, so to speak. And it's getting smarter and more capable in an exponential fashion that is hard to process; yet it is here nonetheless. It will likely disrupt our way of working and engaging, in what will feel like a "sudden" time frame, much like working from home during Covid-19 did; but unlike Covid-19, we can see it's coming, now, from a year or so away. What are companies doing about it today? Writing emails faster? Summarizing call transcripts? Or are we taking steps now as leaders to get ahead of it? In our opinion, it is the CEO's job and responsibility to see this coming change and take action now.

To set up a gen AI R&D Lab, Mollick said the first advice is that it needs to be run by your own people:

> There's latent expertise in every organization. You need to do R&D yourself. The thing I try to get across to organizations is they need to become a radical R&D organization, which they're not used to being. They're used to having R&D done for them by enterprise software companies that do the R&D and then sell them safe versions of the stuff to use. That hopefully gets them four or five percent gains and often just cost cutting, which is a terrible type of gain anyway. They've had R&D driven out of them.

It's something that we have been experiencing and teaching ourselves for years in the general domain of digital transformation. No one knows your business, your brand, your school, your organization, your industry, like you do. The art of great digital transformation comes from connecting dots between your situation (company, products, culture, industry, competition) and the newest technology and trends. It's always way more effective to connect those dots yourself, and in fact it may be necessary. But what's different—and perhaps even more striking—with gen AI is that this time the disruption is happening to the technology itself. To Mollick's point above, the ability to create your own software-based solutions is suddenly within reach. It's no longer about seeing some new technology come around the corner and adopting it, usually in some limited way. This time it's roll your own application and connect every dot to every process. You almost have to have an R&D lab to figure out how to do that. Mollick emphasized this very point. "Every business is going to be different," he said. "I can't tell you the answer. I can tell you we have a general-purpose tool, 'a Swiss Army knife of the mind,' and you got to figure out how to build it for your user, for yourself. Right? And everybody, if you're good at this stuff, has to learn to push it to the limit."

So we wanted to press Mollick a bit about what specific advice he would give leaders on how to set up their own lab in this regard. "It's about fundamental R&D," he said.

It's about internal benchmarking of these AI apps. It's about trying to get ahead of stuff. If you're not trying to build agents internally, like, if you're not doing an R&D effort, that is a major, major effort inside your organization, you're lost. And if you're relying on other people to deliver the stuff for you, you're in trouble. I think one, one of the key disciplines is benchmarking. How far can you get with the systems today? I think it's about pushing things past the point where they're working. I always tell every company, what's your thing that isn't working right now but it's so close that you could taste it like that. You need to have two or three of those.

You need to be building a replacement for your entire organization in the lab with AI and see when it gets good enough to actually pull off the shelf and replace your entire organization. If it doesn't go another way. What bets are you making on a thing that hasn't happened yet?

At the end of the interview, we went over the best case studies of AI first companies we encountered and wrote about, and asked him to comment on those. He remarked that even the best examples today of applied AI apps and pivots (for example, Khan Academy's Khanmigo) have to be pushed even further in their own lab. He points out that with the next generation of AI systems, the system itself will be able to do much (if not all) of what these various wrapper apps can do, as pioneering as they are. His point to us was that even the Khanmigos of the world need to keep moving and keep pushing themselves to figure out what comes next. Mollick again:

> So Khanmigo is a great example of trying to solve the tutor problem with gen AI. On the other hand, you can feel the walls closing in to some extent. We all saw how Sal [Khan] was also the first person to demo "advanced AI voice" with tutoring and "AI vision" with tutoring. And that already shifts what Khanmigo is going to do. And, to take it a step further, if GPT-5 is smarter and can plan better, do you still need the Khanmigo wrapper around it? Like, there's some open questions there about that, right? You see how there's a difference between dynamic processes and static processes?

. . .

If you really think about it, what Mollick was doing was shaking us by the shoulders and saying to us that we were coming right up to the line of being right with our assessment of the AI space and our recommended playbook, but that we were falling short in one critical way. We weren't being strong enough in our recommendations in light of the size of the disruption, opportunity, and change that was speeding toward us all. Mollick said, "If a company isn't doing this now, they are basically lost." And just because it will seem like extreme advice to companies now (given that most don't even have widespread AI literacy or even a decent AI use policy), that doesn't make him wrong. In fact, the more we turned it over in our heads, the more we realized he was right. Ironically, we're ending the book with a holy-shit moment just as we began the book with a holy-shit moment. We were reminded of our walk around the park when Sam Altman told us that AGI would be here in three to five years and that 95 percent of marketing as we know it today will be done by AI within three years. We had spent the last year learning and thinking about what is happening, what is likely to happen, and what to do about it in business, and Mollick was saying you're not thinking big enough. Wow!

When you think about the recommendation that all companies create a gen AI R&D lab *right now*, it's the equivalent of saying that this disruption and innovation that's coming with the next turn of the crank with gen AI is going to be so capable and so substantial that entire elements of the way you run your company will change. If it's really true that the combination of even more intelligence with chain-of-thought reasoning and agentic behavior will allow companies to have almost superhuman executives that can take over certain functions and capabilities, then they will have to take advantage of this and rewire the way they're organized and rewire the way they run their companies. It will be that significant.

That's why Mollick is saying that companies need to actually create a new AI *function* and rewire their organizational structure and processes now, and not wait. Companies and organizations have functions such as operations, marketing, technology, finance, and HR. This would be creating a new function. Adam was reminded of the early days at Starbucks when the concept of digital was an entirely new function, but it took years for companies to figure that out. They just tucked it under technology or marketing, but over time the CDO role became critical, and once companies treated digital strategy and implementation as a separate function, they were able to get real traction.

With gen AI, there is even more of a case that leaders and companies should establish this function now. You're starting to see this with the introduction of AI-officer roles popping up on LinkedIn. The changes and opportunities brought on by the prior technology revolutions (computerization, followed by the internet, and then mobile/social/cloud) took a decade or longer to take hold as they permeated the landscape. The gen AI revolution, to Professor Mollick's point, has the potential to radically change the way we work in a much quicker and more dramatic fashion (that is, over the next twenty-four months).

An AI lab is the only way you could create a new function so quickly. When no one has the training and experience around such a new function, you would have to grab just the right group of nontechnical and technical people, get them really up to speed on AI, and then go experiment, build things, and (most important) learn—learn what current processes and experiences can be automated and improved now, learn what *almost* works now (as Mollick suggests) but will work soon when the AI models and systems improve, and learn what previously impossible breakthroughs might now be possible due to this incredible new "intelligence as a service."

Let's take a hypothetical example. Let's say Starbucks and its new CEO decided to set up a gen AI R&D lab right now. What would it look like? For a global company of Starbucks's size and complexity, it might make sense to set up a dedicated ten-person team for the lab, perhaps split into five two-person teams with access to technical help in terms of building applied AI apps and experimenting with various data schemes and analysis. This team would support a variety of other functions and business lines with its opportunity assessments and experiments. Immediately this team would start tackling the biggest problems facing the company today—the most intractable ones where the traditional methods have not yielded the right results. Take mobile orders and an in-store deployment. This is an area that Starbucks probably would like to get after right now, and it would love to have an entirely new department of intelligence, strategy, and analysis that could absorb the variety of layouts, barista plays, beverage routines, customer flows, and mobile ordering data—to come up with some answers that perhaps the team themselves have not come up with.

. . .

In this one example of just one challenging issue for one area of Starbucks, success can be objectively measured in terms of wait times for mobile orders at peak times at busy stores, in terms of customer-experience scores in these scenarios, in terms of same-store sales (year over year) for these dayparts at these stores, and in terms of barista (Starbucks calls them store "partners") surveys around effectiveness, ease of deployment measures, and production routines. Having access to a superintelligent model and AI system to help solve this challenge and improve these measurable success criteria would at a minimum be helpful and might even be the extra factor that gets the company to get past this challenge overall.

But this is just one example, for just one area in need of improvement. Imagine putting an AI lab up against challenges and opportunities across HR, product development, supply chain, and even brand creative (with synthetic AI-based audiences that the team could test creative against). It made us think, if this is a new function that can and should be applied against every other function and line of business, then it likely raises the question of whether companies and organizations should be creating a new position for chief AI officer.

The short answer is yes. But it's complicated by the fact that this is so new and is moving so fast that you don't want to get delayed and distracted by what would likely be a multimonth process to scope out and bring in an AI leader. We have seen this movie play out too many times; where a company needs a functional overhaul but wants to wait until just the right leader is in place, and thereby loses months of time and opportunity costs. In the case of a chief AI officer, if you have done the requisite education and training of the members of an AI council, and that council has a chairperson, then you have at least an acting chief AI officer in that chairperson, for starters.

So, for the chair of the AI council (or AI champions team) or the like, what does your first one hundred days on the job look like? For starters, if you are like Brice Challamel (Moderna's VP of AI products and platform), you run your own transformational playbook around listening tours, understanding deeply the goals, challenges, and structural issues around every single department of the company; and from there develop a robust program for rolling out AI education and engagement to the whole company, leading to a champions team and the cataloging of use cases. But for most new AI officers (whether chief AI officer or chair of the AI council), the first one hundred days is likely going to be a bit more tactical. Your first one hundred days should have the following goals:

- Make sure there is a scalable AI education and literacy "academy" available to the company in some form, and ensure that a critical mass (at least a core handful of cross-functional leaders; an AI council) has gone through some sort of boot camp and education. (And make sure there is a mandate and mechanism for this group to constantly stay updated on the latest developments in the AI world.)

- Set up an AI use policy, review/update others in existence, and create a mechanism for the AI council to administer this policy on an ongoing basis.

- Create a literal or virtual AI lab made up of either the council itself, or a designated group of other cross-functional team members, whose mandate is both to ensure that a comprehensive AI impact assessment and road-map initiative is underway and being project managed and also to make itself available to each and every function and business unit of the company to help augment problem solving on top challenges and opportunities. This will likely encompass what comes up in the AI impact assessment and road-map process, but is also meant to be available for ad hoc issues that come up (large and small).

- The chief AI officer also needs to do something that is hard to be prescriptive around: they need to be the chief transformational officer of the company for the moment, and that involves being an incredibly good listener, garnering trust and credibility from the entire company. One of Stephen Covey's seven habits is "first seek to understand, and then seek to be understood." It's why Brice Challamel's listening tour at Moderna was so successful. It's the art of being an effective change agent, and it's perhaps the number one success factor in the first one hundred days for anyone in the lead on AI transformation at an organization.

. . .

Our conversation with Mollick, we realized, was the perfect capstone for the book. Mollick reminded us that our journey started with a holy-shit moment and that we should not lose sight that there are more holy-shit moments just around the corner, as this technology is only in phase one on its own journey to AGI status. In this sense, our intuition that this final chapter would feel as much like a reintroduction was correct. It's a reminder of what's coming, and how we need to be thinking about not just the playbook for today, but the playbook that future proofs organizations for tomorrow.

There is an analogy we came up with for how to think about the AI first playbook (which as of this chapter now includes setting up a gen AI R&D lab), and that's the game of tennis. The next wave of gen AI capabilities is coming at us fast, like a tennis ball being hit right at you, zooming over the net, from across the court. It may not be AGI next year, but with the next turn of the crank, we will all likely start to "feel the AGI," and major disruption and opportunities will be present for almost all organizations. You have to be in position, knees bent, ready to hit that ball.

The AI first playbook we have developed thus far in this book is kind of like getting your footwork right in tennis. The ball is coming at you faster than you think. So rather than just standing there with your feet together and your racquet at your side, you need to be moving your feet into position, getting your racquet back. Then you will be in position to hit the ball when it's right in front of you. The playbook isn't an end in itself. It's what you do to be in a position to do the real work—which is experimenting, pushing, moving, and figuring out what can be done now; but more important, figuring out what can be done when the next generation of AI comes out next year. And, yeah, it might be even sooner than that, perhaps later this year.

It also occurred to us that no company is going to be able to build a gen AI R&D lab without first implementing the other elements of the AI first playbook as an initial step. This is true by definition. As Mollick advises, the lab would be staffed by a cross-functional team of internal people who have had the right set of training and education to reach basic AI literacy and proficiency, who would be operating under a clearly understood set of AI use-policy guidelines set up by the right AI council, and who would likely be taking the AI impact-assessment and road-map ideas coming out of the council and experimenting with those and other ideas.

Mollick's advice is the natural extension of the AI first playbook thus far. The playbook is just the first step. Companies have to take the next step (develop an AI lab) on their own, and they need to do it now.

From here, we plan on continuing our AI journey. We will continue compiling examples of AI first companies. How did they set up their lab? What worked? What didn't? Getting to radical productivity lift by adopting AI every day is just table stakes. It gives companies a competitive edge today, but tomorrow it will be a different paradigm: those companies that haven't gotten AI first and set up their lab will risk being obsolete.

CONCLUSION

If we are living our mission from this book project from this point forward, and if you are living the principles we are espousing here, then we will see each other on the trail as we compare notes and get ready for the next chapter together. After this book gets published in hardcover form, we plan on opening up our book-reader community to a broader AI first community around future content that we create in this arena. It turns out that our AI journey is just getting started.

Notes

Introduction

1. Meredith Ringel Morris et al., "Position: Levels of AGI for Operationalizing Progress on the Path to AGI," *Proceedings of the International Conference on Machine Learning*, no. 235 (2024), doi.org/10.48550/arXiv.2311.02462.

Chapter 1

1. Author interview with Reid Hoffman, December 2023.
2. Reid Hoffman with ChatGPT, *Impromptu: Amplifying Our Humanity Through AI* (Anacortes, WA: Dallepedia, 2023).

Chapter 2

1. Author interview with Bill Gates, January 6, 2024.
2. Fabrizio Dell'Acqua et al., "Navigating the Jagged Technological Frontier: Field Experimental Evidence of the Effects of AI on Knowledge Worker Productivity and Quality," Harvard Business School Working Paper, no. 24-013, September 2023.
3. Deloitte, "Now Decides Next: Insights from the Leading Edge of Generative AI Adoption," Deloitte's State of Generative AI in the Enterprise, Quarter One report, January 2024.
4. Boston Consulting Group, "BCG AI Radar: From Potential to Profit with GenAI," January 12, 2024.

Chapter 3

1. Author interview with Jaime Teevan, January 30, 2024.
2. Author interview with Mustafa Suleyman, February 27, 2024.
3. Author interview with Bill Gates, January 6, 2024.
4. Author interview with Eric Vaughan, February 23, 2024.
5. Author interview with Eric Vaughan, February 23, 2024.
6. Author interview with Alicia Parker, March 4, 2024.
7. Author interview with Paul Roetzer, February 14, 2024.

Chapter 5

1. Fabrizio Dell'Acqua et al., "Navigating the Jagged Technological Frontier: Field Experimental Evidence of the Effects of AI on Knowledge Worker Productivity and Quality," Harvard Business School Working Paper, no. 24-013, September 2023.

Chapter 6

1. All quotes in this chapter from Salman Khan come from the authors' interview on July 2, 2024.

Chapter 7

1. From OpenAI's own website (openai.com), which details the partnership and its impact on Moderna's operations. This source, while not a traditional press release, serves as a direct announcement from one of the companies involved.

2. From openai.com.

3. Author interview with Brice Challamel, August 2, 2024.

4. Author interview with Brice Challamel, August 2, 2024.

5. Author interview with Brice Challamel, August 2, 2024.

6. The source of the Harvard/BCG/Ethan Mollick research study is a working paper titled "Navigating the Jagged Technological Frontier: Field Experimental Evidence of the Effects of AI on Knowledge Worker Productivity and Quality." This study was conducted as a collaboration between researchers from Harvard Business School, the Wharton School at the University of Pennsylvania, the University of Warwick, and the MIT Sloan School of Management, in partnership with Boston Consulting Group (BCG).

7. Authors' interview with Moderna.

Conclusion

1. Author interview with Ethan Mollick, September 3, 2024.

Index

Acknowledgments

We would like first and foremost to thank and acknowledge our colleague Rose Kelly, without whom this book and project literally would not have been possible. Rose managed all of our meetings, our research, and our writing schedule, and she set up the book community, doing it all with a professionalism, tenacity, and grace that was world-class. Rose added to the story arc, conclusions, and dot connecting that we tried to do throughout.

We would also like to thank and acknowledge our editor and sponsor for this book and project with Harvard Business Review Press, Scott Berinato. Scott should be given credit for this book even existing, as he was the one who reached out to us, inspiring the book in the first place; and also for being such a talented editor and mentor on the entire process.

We have deep appreciation for our community of readers who have thus far participated in a first-of-its-kind "serialized book + community project" with Harvard Business Review Press. Thank you for taking a chance with us, participating, engaging, and giving us feedback and direction as we put forth each chapter.

And finally, we would love to thank each and every AI leader, technology leader, and business leader who agreed to speak with us on the record for this book. Our AI journey as documented in the

ACKNOWLEDGMENTS

arc of this book happened through a series of connected, thoughtful discussions with these leaders, who sat down with us and gave us their wisdom and advice and told us their own AI-journey stories, so that we could have an opportunity to connect the dots and tell our own story here.

About the Authors

Adam Brotman is an entrepreneur with over twenty-five years of experience leading major tech and consumer brands. He cofounded Forum3 in 2021 to help brands leverage emerging technologies, serving clients like Anheuser-Busch, Crumbl, Starbucks, and Tishman Speyer. Previously, Adam was president, chief experience officer, and co-CEO at J.Crew, where he launched the widely successful J.Crew Rewards program. At Starbucks, he was the inaugural chief digital officer and EVP of global retail operations, developing the payment, ordering, and loyalty platform that amassed sixty million members.

Adam has been recognized as one of *Fast Company*'s "100 Most Creative People" and as CDO Club's CDO of the Year. He serves on the boards of Ruby Tuesday and Cabi and has held board positions at Neiman Marcus Group and Brooks Sports.

He received his bachelor's degree from UCLA and his JD from the University of Washington School of Law. Follow Adam on LinkedIn and X/Twitter, @adambrotman.

Andy Sack is a seasoned entrepreneur and investor with over twenty-five years of experience in tech, finance, and venture capital. Dubbed the "godfather of the Seattle startup community" by Geek-Wire, Andy has been instrumental in building and investing in tech companies that drive innovation. In 2021, Andy cofounded Forum3 to help brands explore and leverage emerging technologies, serving clients such as Anheuser-Busch, Crumbl, Starbucks, and Tishman Speyer. Previously, Andy was a consultant for Microsoft, driving digital transformation under CEO Satya Nadella. Before that, he was managing director of Techstars Seattle, where he led the 2011 cohort to become the highest-performing in the program's history, with seed investments in unicorns like Remitly, Zipline, and Outreach. Andy has also cofounded and exited three successful tech companies to Axciom, the New York Times Digital, and Microsoft.

He received his bachelor's degree from Brown University and his MBA from MIT's Sloan School of Management, and he currently resides in Seattle, Washington. Follow Andy on LinkedIn and X/Twitter, @AndySack.